The Rapture of His Bride

Opening of the Sixth Seal
&
The Blood Moon Cataclysmic Events

Timothy R. Gilbert, MA

Upcoming Books by Timothy Gilbert:

Daniel in the 21st Century-A Novel

Who is the Antichrist?

Hearing the voice of God

Miraculous Faith that moves Mountains

Mercy Is/Mercy Does

Timothy R. Gilbert, MA

The Rapture of His Bride

Opening of the Sixth Seal & The Blood Moon Cataclysmic Events

Suppose Jesus was coming back for a Bride and NOT a Church.?

Copyright © Timothy R Gilbert 2022 All rights reserved. All Content is the property of the author and may NOT be copied or printed for profit. No part of this publication may be reproduced, stored in a retrieval system, or transmitted in any form or by any means—electronic, mechanical, photocopy, recording, or any other—except for brief quotations in printed reviews—without the express written permission by the author.

This is the result of diligent study of the Holy Scriptures and are the author's views. Scriptures used are primarily from the King James Version (KJV) of the Bible unless otherwise noted.

Cover Design, Graphics, and publishing by Timothy R. Gilbert

First Printing 2022

ISBN: 978-0-578-26960-3

Preface

For centuries Christians and theologians alike have been discussing and debating on eschatology— the study of end times. Is there going to be a "Rapture" experience for those in the Church today? When will this experience take place? How do I know that this is real and that I will be one of those who will be raptured? Is the Antichrist coming before or after the Rapture? These questions and more are answered in this book. You will find over 300 direct quotes from the Scriptures. This is on purpose.

Apostle Paul called this union between Christ and His bride a 'great mystery' (Eph. 5:32). He also called the Rapture a great mystery. This means it is NOT easy to understand. Suppose Apostle John actually meant what he said at the outset of the Book of Revelation. "…and he sent and **signified (codified)** *it* by his angel unto his servant John…" (Rev. 1:1). He used certain words on purpose to reveal the meaning of what he was saying.

This book is meant to shine a light on these words and certain passages of Scripture. Some Scriptures will be familiar, others may not. We must not stop pursuing our bridegroom and our Lord Jesus Christ; for our pursuit is not in vain, because He is altogether lovely. In our pursuit we will find ourselves becoming more like Him; and desiring Him more and more, sharing in the bridal cry, "come...even so, come, Lord Jesus." It is, after all, the words of His bride, in the final book of the Word of God.

"And the Spirit and the bride say, Come" (Rev. 22:17).

Acknowledgments

For any author, writing a book is a long journey from start to finish. In this journey you meet people along the way, some by choice, and others by accident…if you believe in accidents.

My first acknowledgement is to Jesus Christ, who changed my life and loved me enough to die for me on a very cruel cross of crucifixion. He IS the reason I am writing this book. I also thank the Holy Spirit for revelation that ONLY He can give.

I would like to thank my wife, Kim, for all her encouragement to finish this book. She knows my flaws and weaknesses, and despite them all she still believes in me.

Clovia Dupuis lovingly volunteered her editing skills. I am so very thankful.

Along the way I met some very wonderful people that endured a class I taught on this subject and friends that heard some 'sound-bites' from this book. Thank you ALL.

Finally, I thank all those that were willing to read and critique this book. I have included their quotes and names on the following page.

Endorsements

"If you've been a Christian for any length of time, no doubt you've heard the word "Rapture" mentioned at some time in a conversation or sermon! That's because this event is a major biblical event spoken of in the Bible. According to many Bible scholars, this event is definitely on the Lord's chronological time table, but has not yet occurred. The Bible refers to this event as an end time or last day's event that all Christians should be anticipating to take place at any moment. Unfortunately many Christians know very little about this event. In my opinion, knowing about and understanding more about "The Rapture" is vital for the health and readiness of every born again believer.

This book you hold in your hand will help you do just that. Tim, who has obviously spent hours studying and prayerfully seeking revelation from God on this subject, will help you get a much better understanding of this end time event called "The Rapture". I believe after reading the pages of this book you'll be infused with hope and be much better equipped to face your glorious future!"

Todd Menard, Former Senior Pastor of Family Life Church, Lafayette, Louisiana

"I have been knowing Tim for several years. He is a man who has a heart for God and his Word. He is both a student and a teacher of the Word of God. He has taught several Bible studies at our church and we have seen the fruit from these studies in our congregation. Tim is very encouraging and he has a desire for people to know Christ more."

Brandon Miller, Senior Pastor of Family Life Church, Lafayette, Louisiana

"Over time there has been thousands and thousands of books written on the topic of the Rapture of the Church. Timothy Gilbert's book, The Rapture of His Bride (Opening of the Sixth Seal And the blood moon cataclysmic events) takes a fresh approach to this topic by connecting Old Testament types, biblical prophecy, and other scriptures to explain this most important topic. I have greatly appreciated Timothy's understanding of the bride of Christ and how intimacy with the bridegroom is key in preparation for this glorious event. I highly recommend this book."

Greg Miller, Author and Founding pastor of Sacred Assembly, Kansas City, Missouri

"The Rapture of His Bride" is a comprehensive look at prophecy and the subject of Christ's bride. I found the book to be an easy read but thorough study that kept my interest throughout from start to finish."

Pastor Jerry Habig, Director of Provident Ministries Network, South Bend, Indiana

Introduction

How important is the Rapture of the Bride of Christ? What difference does it make if I believe that Christ will come for His Bride before the Tribulation, in the midst of the Tribulation, or at the very end of the Tribulation? The timing of His return is critical to our belief in what He said, our understanding in who we are as His bride, and how this changes us in the world we live in.

Does God keep His promises? This is the very first reason we must believe in the Rapture of his bride, because he promised it. It isn't a promise that is hard to believe in; because there is a history of people being snatched from this planet and taken up to God. Enoch was the first, and there are a total of 10 Biblical accounts of this phenomena.

So, what makes the Rapture difficult to accept? Paul gives us the answer. "Behold, I shew you a mystery…" (I Cor. 15:51). The answer is that it is a mystery. According to Webster's definition a mystery is a "religious belief based on divine revelation, especially one regarded as beyond human understanding;" therefore It has to come by the revelation of the Scriptures. It isn't impossible, it just requires humility and willingness to search the Scriptures.

Humility is important to understand mysteries. Jesus told his disciples: "Unto you it is given to know the mystery of the kingdom of God: but unto them that are without, all these things are done in parables" (Mk. 4:11). The Bible shows us that God "resists the proud, but gives grace to the humble" (James 4:6; I Pe. 5:5).

To those that look for Him, He will appear. They will be a bride without spot or wrinkle. They will be a bride that has 'made herself ready.' The teaching of the Rapture of His bride includes planning, watching, and LOVING His appearing. This is a reunion of His bride and the bridegroom, not just a family reunion. It is MOST intimate. The best definition of intimacy that I know of is "into-Him-I-see." He gives us permission to see into Him. It is what the Song of Solomon writes about. "Draw me, we will run after thee: the king hath brought me into his chambers…" (Song 1:4).

In this study we will look at Scriptures that give evidence of this phenomena called the Rapture. We will also look at WHO will be raptured. Jesus is coming back for His bride. He is not coming back for a religious person, or someone who is associated with the Bride, like the 5 foolish virgins, but someone who is 'ready', 'looking', AND 'loving' his appearing.

This study is definitely NOT an exhaustive study. It merely scratches the surface. Hopefully like it was said of the Bereans, it will cause the reader to 'search the scriptures' (Acts 17:10,11). Another hope I have is that those reading this will WANT to have a more intimate relationship with the one that has given his all to us—Jesus Christ. To Him be the glory, the honor, and the majesty because He is worthy.

Lastly, this is NOT a research paper, or a thesis. If it were I would have written references from other writers. Instead, this is an exploration of certain Scriptures and digging deeper into what their meaning is. These are my own findings and are certainly not the end of the study of Scripture, but just the beginning. Hopefully, this book will be a spark, that once fanned, will become a blazing fire in your life and will continue to burn until His arrival.

Table of Contents

The Rapture	5
The Credibility of the Rapture	21
The Timing of the Rapture	37
The Bride of Christ	43
The Seven Churches	57
The First Five Seals	77
The Opening of the Sixth Seal	89
Words Revealing the Rapture	101
Are We Ready?	123
The Reward	129

"He Reveals the Deep and Secret Things: He Knoweth What Is in the Darkness, and the Light Dwelleth With Him" (Daniel. 2:22).

"Surely the Lord GOD Will Do Nothing, but He Reveals his Secret Unto his Servants the Prophets" (Amos 3:7).

"It Is the Glory of God To Conceal a Thing: but the Honor of Kings Is To Search out a Matter" (Proverbs 25:2).

Chapter One

The Rapture

The reader will not find the word "rapture" in the Bible. As such, some people believe that the Idea of the Rapture is NOT Biblical. They could not be more wrong. Several scriptures in the New Testament, written primarily by Paul, support the Idea of the Rapture (1 Cor. 15:51-53; 1 Thess. 2:19; 3:13; 4:13-18; 5:9-11, 23; 2 Thess. 2:1-3). Luke also confirms these scriptures (Lu. 21:35-36; Acts 1:1-11; 8:39-40). The author of Hebrews (Heb. 11:5), James (Jas. 5:7-8); Peter (2 Pe. 3:4-18), and John (John 14:3; 1 John 2:28; 3:2-3; Rev. 3:10; 4:1-2; 7:9-17; 12:1-5) also support this teaching. Jesus (Acts 1:2-11), Enoch (Gen 5:24), Elijah (2 Kgs. 2:1-11), and Moses also support the Idea (Mt. 17:3; Mk. 9:4).   Let us not forget that the concept of the Rapture ALSO includes the resurrection of 'the dead' as well as the translation of those still living.

Therefore, if all these people wrote about the Rapture and had these experiences, and passed down through the generations; we should take this subject seriously.

The Patristic Fathers were premillennialists (up to and including the First Ecumenical Council at Nicea in 325). Their premillennial view did not begin to change until Origen in the late third century and did not entirely change until Augustine's doctrine became the orthodox view of the Church in the early fifth century.

Although the reader will not find the word "rapture" in the Bible, the Latin word "rapiemur" is in the Latin Vulgate Bible. This word is the equivalent of "caught up" found in Scripture. The word means "we shall be caught up" and was taken from the Greek verb ἁρπάζω (harpazo), meaning "to seize upon, spoil, snatch away or take to oneself," (Acts 8:39; 2 Cor. 12:2, 4; 1 Thess. 4:17; Rev. 12:5). Harpazo is translated "caught up" or "caught away" the five times (out of thirteen) it appears in the Bible. This same theme of God's "deliverance from His wrath," through the "salvation of the Lord Jesus," is spoken of in I Thess. 5:9,10;

"For God has not appointed us to wrath, but unto salvation through our Lord Jesus Christ. who died for us, that whether we wake or sleep, we should live together with Him." (I Thess. 5:9,10).

This verse is commonly quoted by Pastors to illustrate Salvation. If you take this verse in CONTEXT and read the verses surrounding it; you come up with another interpretation. These words are connected to the Rapture previously mentioned in chapter 4 by the words, "that whether we are awake or asleep, we may live together with Him." Paul ties all this together in verse 23; where he says, "now may the God of peace Himself sanctify you entirely and may your spirit and soul and body be preserved complete . . . at the "coming" (parousia) of our Lord Jesus Christ."

The reader should note that Apostle Paul is praying that the ENTIRE Spirit, Soul, and BODY be preserved (to keep one in the state in which he is) blameless ('uncensored' used ONLY in this epistle and used in the context of His coming ALL three times).

*"Ye are witnesses, and God also, how holily and justly and **unblameably** we behaved ourselves among you that believed...for what is our hope, or joy, or crown of rejoicing? Are not even ye in the presence of our Lord Jesus Christ **at his coming**" (I Thess. 2:10,19).*

*"To the end He may stablish your hearts **unblameable** in holiness before God, even our Father, **at the coming of our Lord Jesus Christ** with all His saints" (I Thess. 3:13).*

"And the very God of peace sanctify you wholly; and I pray God your whole spirit and soul and body be

preserved **blameless unto the coming of our Lord Jesus Christ**" *(I Thess. 5:23).*

In I Thess. 5:23, we should understand that Paul is speaking of the Rapture. If he chooses and selects these specific Greek words relating to our Spirit, soul, AND BODY, this alone should tip off those who believe that it is only a "Spiritual" experience and not a physical one. Paul specifically spoke of "corruption" taking on "incorruption." The physical decay of the body (corruption) will transform into a 'new' body raptured into 'newness' of life.

"Now this I say, brethren, that flesh and blood cannot inherit the kingdom of God; neither doth corruption inherit incorruption. Behold, I shew you a mystery; We shall not all sleep, but we shall all be changed, In a moment, in the twinkling of an eye, at the last trump: for the trumpet shall sound, and the dead shall be raised incorruptible, and we shall be changed. For this corruptible must put on incorruption, and this mortal must put on immortality" (I Cor. 15:50-53).

The Rapture/the Return of Christ

There is a difference between the Rapture and the Return of Christ. It is critical to know the verses that pertain to each one. Why is it important to keep the

Rapture and the Second Coming as separate and distinct events?

> *(1) If they are the same event, believers will have to go through the Tribulation. Even though they are promised to be delivered from it. (1 Thessalonians 5:9; Revelation 3:10).*
> *(2) If the Rapture and the Second Coming are the same event, the return of Christ is not imminent, meaning there are things which must occur first (Matthew 24:4-30).*
> *(3) It would not be consistent with the narrative in describing the Tribulation period; because John doesn't mention the church in Revelation chapters 6-19.*

Why is Jesus coming back twice?

The first time He comes back for His Bride. The second time He comes back WITH His Bride. Jesus knows how to treat a lady. His bride is NOT going to go through the Tribulation simply because she is His Bride.

It is true that God's people have gone through times of persecution; but this is not persecution, this is the wrath of man and the wrath of God. It is also true that God brings affliction on His people so that they can learn from it. God had Israel go through the wilderness to humble them.

*"And thou shalt remember all the way which the LORD thy God led thee these forty years in the wilderness, to **humble** thee, and to prove thee, to know what was in thine heart, whether thou wouldest keep his commandments, or no" (Deu. 8:2).*

David said that he was afflicted so that he would learn God's statutes.

*"It is good for me that I have been **afflicted**; that I might learn thy statutes" (Psa. 119:70)*

In both of these cases the goal was to bring about humility. The Bride that Jesus speaks of IS humble. She is one that has kept His commandments (Rev. 3:10). So there is absolutely no purpose in bringing persecution or affliction on her. She is one that has ALREADY gone through the tests and trials. Before God she has been tried and is as pure gold.

His Bride is seen as pure gold. The Candlesticks were made of PURE Gold. Everything in the Holy Place was covered in gold. The City, called the New Jerusalem, and His Bride, is pure gold (Rev. 21:18).

When it comes to the Rapture, deliverance is included in the package. This is because God has a long-standing practice of saving His people before pouring out His wrath, as He did for Noah and Lot. Jesus spoke of both: "In the days of Lot" (Lu. 17:28); and the "days of Noah" (Matt.

24:37). Both were saved from impending doom. They were not told about it and left to deal with it; God rescued them from it. For this reason, Jesus used these two examples when speaking of the end.

> *"For as in the days that were before the flood they were eating and drinking, marrying and giving in marriage, until the day that Noe entered into the ark, And knew not until the flood came, and took them all away; so shall also the coming of the Son of man be" (Mt. 24:38).*

> *"Likewise also as it was in the days of Lot; they did eat, they drank, they bought, they sold, they planted, they builded; But the same day that Lot went out of Sodom it rained fire and brimstone from heaven, and destroyed them all" (Lu. 17:28,29).*

There are specific and distinct differences between the two events. As you can see in the chart below, Scriptures have a different description for each event. I am only showing seven things that are different, but I have heard of as many as twenty or more differences in Scripture.

The Rapture/The Return of Christ

The Rapture	The Return of Christ
Jesus coming for His Bride. (I Thess 4:14-17)	Jesus coming with His Bride. (Rev 19:7-8)
Jesus comes in the air (I Thess 4:13)	Jesus comes to the earth (Zech 14:4)
Appears to His Bride only. (Jn. 11:40)	Every eye will see him (Rev 1:7; Zech 12:10)
Jesus descends with a shout (I Thess 4:16)	Jesus descends with the sword (Rev 19:11)
Only the Bride is seen (I Thess. 4:13-18)	The Bride and others are seen (Rev 19:11)
The dead are raised to Life (I Thess 4:13)	The Living are sent to death (Rev 19:11)
The Bride goes from earth to heaven	The Bride comes from heaven to earth

Some Christians prefer to wait for His Return; others, as well as this author believe He is coming for His Bride first and then return with her when He returns and every eye sees Him.

A Personal Promise to his Bride

The teaching of the Rapture is NOT the creation of a man, as some suggest, but it is the promise from one who wants to come back and take His bride home. It is a promise to those who are "in Christ." It is a catching away of a bride adorned for her husband. She is 'ready', 'watching', and 'loving' His appearing. Some would suggest that the Rapture first occurred in people's minds

AFTER the teachings of the Apostles and therefore is NOT to be taken seriously. They suggest that the Rapture is a byproduct of John Nelson Darby in the time of the 1,800s or because of Schofield's Bible or Hal Lindsey. Neither of these originated the Idea of the Rapture; they merely accentuated it. It was there in the Scriptures all along.

This study is not to refute others, nor is it based on the opinions of others. It is an attempt to honestly look at scriptures and try to fully understand the meaning of these scriptures and the truth they hold regarding the Rapture.

The promise of His coming back for a bride, is also a promise of keeping her from the wrath that is to come. Paul did not say that it was just the wrath of God. He said that we were not appointed unto wrath, but delivered from it. That would mean even the wrath of man, or the Antichrist. It was a promise to be delivered from the Tribulation that would come upon the whole earth (Rev. 3:10).

This would mean that He is not coming in the middle of the Tribulation, but He is coming before the Tribulation begins. We will look further into this in the chapters ahead.

We see subtle hints in the Scriptures to reveal to us confirmations of the point I am making. Perhaps there is something to the way Apostle John worded things when John was addressing the Church in the Book of Revelation and when he was writing about the appearance of the beast in Revelation chapter 13.

Before the Tribulation:

"*He that hath an ear, let him hear what the Spirit saith unto the churches*" *(Rev. 2:7,11,19,29; 3:6,13,22).*

God wrote these words to ALL of the Churches.

During the Tribulation:

"*If any man have an ear, let him hear*" *(Rev. 13:9).*

In contrast, these words God wrote AFTER the Antichrist came. Notice the difference and the words that are NOT present. "...what the Spirit saith unto the churches."

Why? Because neither the Spirit nor His Bride is present during the Tribulation.

Apostle Paul made it clear how the Antichrist would come.

"*For this lawlessness is already at work secretly, and it will remain secret until the one who is holding it back steps out of the way. Then the man of lawlessness will be revealed,*" *(II Thess. 2:7,8) (NLT).*

When the Rapture occurs, the Holy Spirit steps out of the way and makes room for the Antichrist to come.

The KJV of the Bible translates "steps out of the way" as:

"Be taken out of the way...."

The Greek word used here is γίνομαι (ginomai) which Strong's Concordance identifies in this manner:

*"γίνομαι (gínomai), ghin'-om-ahee; a prolongation and middle voice form of a primary verb; to cause to be ("gen"-erate), i.e. (reflexively) to become (come into being), used with great latitude (literal, figurative, intensive, etc.):—**arise**, be assembled, be(-come, -fall, -have self), be brought (to pass), (be) come (to pass), continue, be divided, draw, be ended, fall, be finished, follow, be found, be fulfilled, + God forbid, grow, happen, have, be kept, be made, **be married**, be ordained to be, partake, pass, be performed, be published, require, seem, be showed."*

One day we will be "changed" or, as noted above, "assembled," "arise," and be "married." It is intriguing to note that this SAME word is used by John in Revelation 6:12 three times when describing the appearance of the earthquake, the sun, and the blood moon. John does not use this Greek word again. The author believes that as

Strong indicates 'great latitude' used with this word, it WAS used by John figuratively in Revelation 6:12 on purpose with the same latitude. Paul used it when describing the Spirit being 'taken out of the way,' and John used it here in Revelation 6:12.

John concludes this chapter with those who were witnesses:

"For the great day of His wrath is come" (Rev. 6:17).

This wrath is the same 'wrath' that Paul referred to in I Thess. 5:9,10 and assuring that we were NOT appointed (or made) for wrath, but instead we are saved from it.

There is a multitude spoken of in Revelation chapter 7. From where did this multitude come? The Elder who spoke in Revelation 7 wanted John to know that these came "out of, or from" the Tribulation. This word 'out' is spoken of in great detail by Strong. He said,

*"ἐκ ek, ek; a primary preposition denoting origin (the point whence action or motion proceeds), from, out (of place, time, or cause; literal or figurative; direct or remote)— Also, it denotes **exit or emission out of, as separation from, something with which there has been close connection**."*

In this instance, John uses this word like Apostle Paul used in II Thess. 2:7 in referring to the Spirit being 'taken out.' We will one Day be separated from this earth that we once had a 'close connection' to and taken 'from' it.

The use of these words is NOT by accident and understanding these Greek words gives us a better picture of what John was saying.

When attending Bible College, the Greek class that Dr. Nathan Hann taught was very enlightening. He stressed that the Greek language intends to 'paint a picture.' He said, "it is a picture language, and the outcome of translation is to see that picture." A person needs more than a literal translation to understand the Greek language. When a painter paints a picture, different colors and hues reveal the final product to us. When we take these words and see how the authors use them from the different passages of Scripture and authors, we can ascertain the Scripture's meaning that there is "no private interpretation" when it comes to the Scriptures.

"Knowing this first, that no prophecy of the scripture is of any private interpretation" (II Pe. 1:20).

As a special note, Peter, just four verses earlier, spoke in the context of His coming:

*"For we have not followed cunningly devised fables, when we made known unto you the power and **coming of our Lord Jesus Christ**..." (II Pe. 1:16).*

There is another consideration for the belief in the Rapture, and although it is not the discovery of the author, he does have respect for him. The Idea surrounds the following Scripture and the words "falling away."

"Let no man deceive you by any means: for that day shall not come, except there come a falling away first, and that man of sin be revealed, the son of perdition" (II Thess. 2:3).

Greek scholar, Kenneth Wuest, said, "The words *falling away* are an interpretation of the Greek word, not a translation." The early English translations of the Bible did not translate *apostasia* as "falling away." They translated it as "departure." Coverdale, Tyndale, and the Geneva Bibles, some of the oldest English translations available, translate the word as: "departure," not "falling away." "Apostasy" does not necessarily mean a departure from the faith. The New Testament found this Greek word for apostasy only two times. It is found here and in Acts 21:21, where there is a reference to the Jews forsaking the teachings of Moses.

If we read this verse as Coverdale and Tyndale translated it we have:

> "let no one deceive you by any means, for the day of the Lord will not come unless the departure comes first" (II Thess. 2:3) [TYN, GEN, COV]

What is the departure? Could it be possible that the writer of 1 Thessalonians was talking about the Rapture? The pertinent question is, the departure of what or who? I believe this speaks of the departure of the Bride. Notice the outcome of this departure, *"the man of sin is revealed, the son of perdition"* (II Thess. 2:3). Could verse three and seven be saying the same thing?

> "For the mystery of lawlessness is already at work; only He who now restrains will do so until He is taken out of the way. And then the lawless one will be revealed" (II Thess. 2:7–8).

Something happens in verse 7 that results in the same thing after the event in verse 3. After the departure in verse 3, the Antichrist rises to power.

In verse 7, most commentators agree that *"He* who restrains until *He* is taken away" refers to the Holy Spirit. The Holy Spirit, of course, inhabits the Bride, the body of Christ. Jesus said that we were the light of the world. So it makes sense that darkness cannot overcome the light. The devil is in darkness, so the Antichrist can only move in darkness. For him to come to power, the light has to be gone. We, as His Bride, cannot be here when the Antichrist rules in power. A departure occurs in verse 3, after which the man of sin comes to power. Perhaps the most unambiguous statement in support of the pretribulation position in the Bible IS II Thessalonians 2:1-8.

Finally, it may surprise people that those who still believe in the Rapture are in the minority; and more Churches believe in ONLY the second and final return of Christ. Churches such as Catholics, Eastern Orthodox, Anglicans, Episcopalians, Lutherans, Presbyterians, United Methodists, the United Church of Christ, and most Reformed Christians do not generally use Rapture as a specific theological term, nor do they generally subscribe to the premillennial dispensational views associated with its use.

It may also surprise people that more parishioners believe in the Rapture than their own Pastors. Some pastors feel that Salvation is the ONLY topic to preach.

*"**All scripture** is given by inspiration of God, and is profitable for doctrine, for reproof, for correction, for instruction in righteousness" (II Tim. 3:16).*

Chapter Two

The Credibility of the Rapture

As written earlier, Apostle Paul's writes:

"For the Lord Himself shall descend from heaven with a shout, with the voice of the archangel, and with the trump of God: and the dead in Christ shall rise first: Then we which are alive and remain shall be caught up (raptus) together with them in the clouds, to meet the Lord in the air: and so shall we ever be with the Lord" (I Thess. 4:16,17).

According to Webster's Dictionary, the word AS A NOUN means: "often capitalized: the final ascension of Christians into heaven during the end-times according to Christian theology." As a verb, it is to be "caught away." The same word that Apostle Paul used in the Scriptures. Paul only had the Old Testament to study and learn from at the time of writing. We have the benefit of both the Old Testament and the New Testament. It was not difficult for

Paul to believe the Rapture concept because the Old Testament alludes to it. So far, we have recorded five main accounts of this phenomenon in the Bible. Jewish tradition cites many more possibilities.

Even if there were only one example in Scripture, it should be enough to convince the strongest doubter that the Rapture could be a reality with God.

Five prominent people in the Bible had a 'raptured' experience. So it is not as if it is happening for the first time.

There are, of course, more examples, but these examples are the ones people are most familiar.

1. Enoch (Genesis 5:22-24)
2. Moses (Visibly seen in the Mt of Transfiguration in Mt. 17:3; Mk. 9:4)
3. Elijah (II Kings 2:11) Was in a whirlwind.
4. Jesus Christ. After His resurrection, His disciples saw him raptured.
5. Apostle John (Rev. 4:1,2). He went up to Heaven to receive the vision.

There are enough accounts in the Bible to give weight to this doctrine.

Another reason some people do NOT believe in the Rapture because Jesus never brings it up. He speaks of the Bride of Christ in several parables and stories but does not explicitly address the Rapture. Why? This Revelation was not given to Jesus but to Apostle Paul, who came after Jesus Christ. Jesus was living during the Jewish dispensation, and Paul was not. Other prophets alluded to it, but Apostle Paul was particular. Here is an example of an Old Testament prophet speaking of what Apostle Paul saw.

> "Thy dead men shall live, together with my dead body shall they arise. Awake and sing, ye that dwell in dust: for thy dew is as the dew of herbs, and the earth shall cast out the dead. Come, my people, enter thou into thy chambers, and shut thy doors about thee: hide thyself as it were for a little moment, until the indignation be over past. For, behold, the LORD cometh out of His place to punish the inhabitants of the earth for their iniquity: the earth also shall disclose her blood, and shall no more cover her slain" (Isa. 26:20,21).

What Paul and John saw by Revelation was prophesied in Isaiah. When a person finds Revelation in the New Testament, rest assured that God put it in the Old Testament. It is like the old saying, "The Old Testament is the New Testament concealed, and the New Testament is the Old Testament revealed." Just like Peter spoke, "Knowing this first, that no prophecy of the Scripture is of any private interpretation" (II Pe. 1:20). The words, 'private interpretation' would be translated as 'of one's own unloosing.' In other words, someone else would have spoken of it earlier, either in parable or prophecy. The narrative would have been confirmed elsewhere in Scripture. Here, Isaiah speaks of the dead rising and 'His people going into a chamber until the Day of indignation passes. Jesus also spoke of the door being 'closed' when speaking of the bridal reception. We will see later that not only does Isaiah speak of the event but also when this will occur in God's prophetic timeline.

For some, the Idea of the Rapture is not the problem, it is the timing of the Rapture. Some believe that Jesus will come, but NOT before the Tribulation happens. They use Noah as an example. He went through floods and storms, and God rescued him AFTER the flood. This example may seem like a good argument for believing in post-tribulation rapture theology; however, a person would have to discard the Scripture about being delivered from His wrath. "For God has not appointed us to wrath..." (I Thess. 5:9). I would also point out that Noah went through the flood by staying ABOVE the waters, NOT by being in the water. In other words, Noah prepared a boat, not a submarine.

Those who believe in this teaching are "amillennialists." One reason they do not believe in the Rapture is that they feel that the Church is the world's answer to the destruction that comes upon the earth, and if the Church is NOT here, then the world has no hope. Also, they believe that the Church cannot be overcome and only gets more substantial and significant, so the thousand-year reign is NOT literal, but it is symbolic of a time in which the

Church has come into its own, and its glory shines before the nations. They also believe that the Antichrist has already come, and we are now living in the kingdom age. They believe there is no rapture because there is no reason to take the Church away. They also believe that the new earth and new Heaven described in Isaiah 60 is this kingdom on the earth.

They also believe that Matthew 24 reveals that everything spoken by Jesus is fulfilled in the 40 years of that period, including the Temple's destruction in AD 70. They conclude that the words Jesus spoke, "all these things shall be fulfilled in THIS generation," refers exhaustively to all the things Jesus spoke, and therefore they are completely fulfilled already. The Antichrist has come; the Tribulation is here, while God's wrath pours out. We are now living in the golden age of the Church. This teaching is so full of error that I am surprised that it still exists today.

In the Nicean Council, 318 Bishops went on record as believing in the literal millennial reign of Christ. The root of amillennialism gained momentum when the 'universal Church' (Catholicism) suggested that there could not be any more amazing body on the earth than their Church. The Scriptures do not teach that the Church gets greater but that the 'glory of the Lord' does. He gets greater. Jesus is the King of Kings and Lord of Lords. He is the 'mountain that fills the earth,' not the Church. This heresy has caused the orthodoxy of the Church to be very unclear in the matter of eschatology or the Study of End Times. So what should we believe? It is NOT by accident that Jesus spoke these words at the end of His answer to the question, "when will the end come?":

"Heaven and earth shall pass away, but my words shall not pass away" (Matt. 24:35).

The solution is His Word. Believe His WORD!

Today, only 1 out of 4 Christians believe in the literal Rapture of the Church BEFORE the Tribulation. Some believe it will happen, but only after we first go through 3.5 yrs of Tribulation. They are commonly called "mid-tribbers." Some believe that there will be a rapture AFTER the Tribulation is complete. The author contends that a Christian should believe that her bridegroom is coming for her BEFORE the Tribulation begins.

When the author was attending Bible College, he heard a visiting preacher address the topic of the Rapture. At this time, the Idea popped up that the Church would go THROUGH the Tribulation just like Noah went through the flood. Many followed this logic. As it gained traction, those still convinced that the Bride would be snatched away BEFORE the Tribulation were asked to defend their position. This noted prophetic teacher was asked what he thought about the Bride going through the Tribulation. He replied:

"All I know is: THAT is no way to treat a lady."

The author believes he is right. Remember, Jesus is coming back for His Bride. Why would He want His Bride to suffer wrath when He already took on wrath for her? It is more biblical to believe that she is going to be snatched away FROM the Tribulation than it is to believe that she will go THROUGH the Tribulation (The evidence points to WHY there is a rapture rather than IF there is a rapture). It is Biblical to believe in the Bride's and the Bridegroom's union in the air.

The King of Kings will crown His queen. He is crowning her at His appearing. It will be enough if all we have to believe in is Apostle Paul's letters in 1 Corinthians 15 and 1 Thessalonians 4.

The Last Trump

Some people have pointed out that the Scripture says He will come at the 'last' trumpet sound and that this is about the trumpets that sound in the book of Revelation. That would mean that the Rapture is at the 'end' of the Tribulation. Let us look at this 'last' trump spoken of by Paul.

*"In a moment, in the twinkling of an eye, at the **last trump**: for the trumpet shall sound, and the*

dead shall be raised incorruptible, and we shall be changed" (I Cor. 15:52).

Different trumpets were used in the Old Testament, each having its purpose. The shofar sounded for one purpose, and the silver trumpets sounded for another.

"Make thee two trumpets of silver; of a whole piece shalt thou make them: that thou shalt use them for the calling of the assembly, and for the journeying of the camps" (Nu. 10:2).

These silver trumpets were given to Hazael, king of Syria, by Joash, the king of Judah, in exchange for their lives (II Ki. 12:18). These silver trumpets were NEVER replaced. From that time on, the shofar was the only trumpet used. This trumpet sounded during Jubilee, the Day of Atonement, and at assembly time.

The key here is that Apostle Paul went out of his way to use the words "at the last trump" instead of "trumpet." He wanted to distinguish the two. The last trumpet to sound in the Bible is the seventh trumpet in the book of Revelation.

The word "last" also means "the last in succession." The Day of atonement or the "feast of trumpets" sounded the shofars 100 times, and then after the last trump sounded, the feast began. The trumpets blew, after which the walls of Jericho fell, and this 'last' trump speaks of something happening AFTER the trumpet sounds. Apostle Paul is suggesting the same thing here. He said, "for the trumpet shall sound," and then the dead in Christ shall rise.

Just as the feast begins on the Day of atonement at the "last trump," the Rapture begins at the "last trump" Apostle Paul speaks. The words "last trump" means something different than "trumpet" AND a tip-off to the timing of the Rapture or the season thereof (the season of trumpets or ingathering).

Matthew 24

Matthew 24 is another passage of Scripture where some people get confused. After all, if Jesus did not make it clear, then why should we believe it? Jesus was always clear about what He said. The answer lies in whom Jesus was addressing and the time in which Jesus lived. His voice was to the Jews; Paul's voice was to the Gentiles. The Rapture, Paul revealed, not Jesus. Why? The Revelation came AFTER the manifestation of the Holy Spirit on the Day of Pentecost (Acts 2:1-21). After this manifestation, Peter refers to the prophet Joel. The latter part of his quote shows us the same thing Apostle John saw in Revelation 6:12.

> *"The sun shall be turned into darkness, and the moon into blood, before that great and notable day of the Lord come" (Acts 2:20).*

"And I beheld when he had opened the sixth seal, and, lo, there was a great earthquake; and the sun became black as sackcloth of hair, and the moon became as blood..." (Rev. 6:12).

Acts 2:21 is commonly understood to be a call for Salvation. Is this true?

"And it shall come to pass, that whosoever shall call on the name of the Lord shall be saved" (Acts 2:21).

Remember this verse is a direct quote from Joel 2:32, which states:

*"And it shall come to pass, that whosoever shall call on the name of the LORD shall **be delivered**: for in mount Zion and in Jerusalem shall be deliverance, as the LORD hath said, and **in the remnant whom the LORD shall call**." (Joel 2:32).*

In context, this is NOT about the Salvation experience, but in deliverance from something that comes to pass. When a person looks at the verse and breaks down the Greek words, they can see something entirely different. For instance, the words "shall call on" in Greek are:

"to invoke, adore, worship, the Lord)." [STRONG].

"...shall be saved" according to Strongs is:

"to save, to keep safe and sound, to rescue from danger or destruction; to save and transport into" (STRONG).

Putting this together, Peter says, "they that adore and worship the Lord shall be kept safe and sound, rescued from danger or destruction and transported." He must be referring to the Rapture.

Here in Matthew 24, before the coming of the Holy Spirit, we find Jesus addressing the question of the sign of His coming. To which coming are they referring? It is the 2nd coming, NOT the Rapture.

> "And as He sat upon the mount of Olives, the disciples came unto Him privately, saying, Tell us, when shall these things be? and what shall be the sign of thy coming, and of the end of the world?" (Matt. 24:3).

Note where Jesus was sitting? He was sitting on the Mount of Olives. The Mount of Olives is where Jesus returns, so this discourse has to do with His return, not the Rapture. To be clear, the Rapture of the Bride of Christ is when He comes FOR His Bride, and the return of Christ is when He comes back WITH His Bride and steps foot on the Mount of Olives.

"And His feet shall stand in that day upon the mount of Olives..." (Zech. 14:4).

This conversation was private, not public, and pointed toward Jewish life. It all started with the discussion of the destruction of the Jewish Temple. Jesus is speaking to His disciples regarding the outcome of Jewish, NOT Christian life.

As Christian, we can glean from what Jesus is saying, but He is NOT speaking of His Bride but the Jewish community. He is living in a different Dispensation than Paul.

Jesus replies, "And Jesus answered and said unto THEM, Take heed that no man deceive YOU" (Mt. 24:4). Jesus is not referring to anyone else. Jesus is giving THEM a timeline involving the Jewish people. They have been awaiting a Messiah for centuries, and Jesus knew that one day a person would stand in the Holy Place and declare himself to be God and that long-awaited Meshiach or Messiah of the Jews would present himself. Surrounding the coming of this false christ is what this is all about. Jesus begins with, "Take heed that no man deceives YOU."

Moreover, saying to them, "For many shall come in my name, saying, I am Christ; and shall deceive many" (Mt. 24:5). He then gives a discourse about what will happen BEFORE the Antichrist comes and AFTER he comes. He is warning the Jewish community that one day, speaking of the Temple (Jewish), it would be utterly destroyed and restored so that the Antichrist could step up to proclaim himself to be Christ. The Bible calls him the Antichrist, and he will deceive many people when he comes, especially the Jews.

Notice what Jesus tells them when He says the end will come:

> "But he that shall endure unto the end, the same shall be saved" (Mt. 24:13).

Jesus gives us a clear timeline later repeated in Revelation chapter 6 when the first seals open. The four horsemen or the first four seals are what Jesus refers to as the 'beginning of sorrows,' or the beginning of birth pains. The author contends that the beginning of sorrow has already come, and the four horses are already riding. The recent release of plagues brought death to millions of people on this earth. Matthew 24 illustrates these times and further the times after. They are also known as "Jacob's Trouble." The world is going to realize that the time has come.

> "For the great day of His wrath is come; and who shall be able to stand" (Rev. 6:17)?

Some people have suggested that the following words of Jesus suggest the Rapture:

"Then shall two be in the field; the one shall be taken, and the other left. Two women shall be grinding at the mill; the one shall be taken, and the other left" (Matt. 24:40,41).

"I tell you, in that night there shall be two men in one bed; the one shall be taken, and the other shall be left. Two women shall be grinding together; the one shall be taken, and the other left. Two men shall be in the field; the one shall be taken, and the other left. And they answered and said unto Him, Where, Lord? And He said unto them, Wheresoever the body is, thither will the eagles be gathered together" (Lu. 17:34-37).

Notice that Jesus speaks these words AFTER the Antichrist is revealed just before the Armageddon battle. These references are said AFTER Jesus warns them to flee to the mountains. Those who did not flee were left to suffer. Flee from what or who? Jesus may be referring to those taken by the Antichrist, not the honest Christ.

So when a person looks at this chronologically, they see it as more straightforward.

1. Jerusalem Temple destroyed (Matt. 24:2).
2. Beginnings of sorrows (v. 4-8).
3. Persecution and worldwide hatred for the Jews (v. 9).
4. Betrayal among the Jewish people (v. 10).

5. The false prophet arises (v. 11).
6. Lawlessness leads to cold love (v. 12).
7. Worldwide preaching of the Gospel (v. 14).
8. The Antichrist stands in the Holies of Holies, declaring he is G-d, or the Meshiach (v. 15).
9. Fleeing the Antichrist (v.16-20).
10. Tribulation begins (v.21,22).
11. The false prophet and the Antichrist continue to deceive even the elect of G-d.
12. Battle of Armageddon (v. 28)

Birth Pains

When we see the connection of the "beginning of sorrows" or "birth pains'"with the progression to the Rapture, we see viability. It appears in the prophetic books, as seen in Isaiah:

"Like as a woman with child, that draweth near the time of her delivery, is in pain, and crieth out in her pangs; so have we been in thy sight, O LORD. We have been with child, we have been in pain, we have as it were, brought forth wind; we have not wrought any deliverance in the earth; neither have the inhabitants of the world fallen. Thy dead men shall live, together with my dead body shall they arise. Awake and sing, ye that dwell in dust; for thy dew is as the dew of herbs, and the earth shall cast out the dead. Come, my people,

enter thou into thy chambers, and shut thy doors about thee: hide thyself as it were for a little moment, until the indignation be overpast. For, behold, the LORD cometh out of his place to punish the inhabitants of the earth for their iniquity: the earth also shall disclose her blood, and shall no more cover her slain" (Isa. 26:17-21).

Jesus confirmed this in Matthew chapter 24:

"All these are the beginning of sorrows (GR. "Birthing pains")

Apostle John also spoke of the first five seals opened. The first four seals describe what Jesus described, then the fifth seal describes the souls slain, and the sixth seal opened, and we have the cataclysmic events happening and, at the same time, the Rapture of His Bride. We will cover more of this in the chapters to follow.

Although Jesus never brings it up, we see it in Apostle Paul's writings. We see it brought up in the writings of the original fathers of the Church and subsequently in their disciples. This Idea has been carried down in other people's writings and characterized in movies. The left behind series is an example. Can so many people be wrong?

Chapter Three

The Timing of the Rapture

Are we allowed to know when the Rapture will occur? The answer is YES and NO. We cannot know the day or the hour in which Jesus comes back because even Jesus does not know. ONLY His Father knows that moment. Remember that Jesus is coming back for His BRIDE. According to Jewish tradition, the groom leaves the Bride after the wedding ceremony to prepare her a place to live. The Bride anxiously awaits for Him to return and snatch her away. He prepares a place while she prepares her person.

"...*his wife hath made herself ready*" *(Rev. 19:7)*

"*That he might present it to Himself a glorious church not having spot, or wrinkle, or any such thing; but that it should be holy and without blemish*" *(Eph. 5:27).*

When the place is complete and the Father is pleased, He speaks to His Son and tells Him, "go and snatch away your bride." So, we cannot know the exact day or hour. Jesus tells us to watch, for no man knows the day or hour.

"But of that day and that hour knoweth no man, no, not the angels which are in heaven, neither the Son, but the Father. Take ye heed, watch and pray: for ye know not when the time is" (Mk. 13:32).

So, the answer is a resounding NO for the exact time the Rapture will take place. We can, however, be sure of the times and the seasons. It is as clear as day.

"Ye are all the children of light, and the children of the day: we are not of the night, nor of darkness" (I Thess. 5:5).

We do not have an appointment for the Tribulation but have been "saved" from the wrath to come.

"For God hath not appointed us to wrath, but to obtain salvation by our Lord Jesus Christ, Who died for us... Wherefore comfort yourselves together, and edify one another, even as also ye do" (I Thess. 5:1-11).

Paul just finished speaking of the Rapture of the Church in chapter 4. He is continuing the discussion beginning here in chapter 5. In the original writings, there were NO chapters but just a continual thought. So, if we link the two together, we have this:

"For the Lord Himself shall descend from heaven with a shout, with the voice of the archangel, and with the trump of God: and the dead in Christ shall rise first: Then we which are alive and remain shall be caught up together with them in the clouds, to meet the Lord in the air: and so shall we ever be with the Lord. Wherefore comfort one another with these words. But of the times and the seasons, brethren, ye have no need that I write unto you" (I Thess. 4:16-5:1).

We can know through the power obtained by the Holy Spirit. Apostle John said as much when he wrote the book of Revelation.

"John to the seven Churches which are in Asia: Grace be unto you, and peace, from Him which is, and which was, and which is to come; and from the seven Spirits which are before His throne" (Rev. 1:4).

The seven spirits are the completeness or perfection of the Holy Spirit. It is believed among most scholars that this is also referenced in Isaiah, referring to the completeness of the Holy Spirit on Jesus Christ.

"And the spirit of the LORD shall rest upon Him, the spirit of wisdom and understanding, the spirit of counsel and might, the spirit of knowledge and of the fear of the LORD" (Isa. 11:2).

The disciples were endowed with the same completeness of the Holy Spirit when God baptized them. The Holy Spirit is the key to understanding the times and the seasons. The Holy Spirit reveals the Son, and the Son reveals the Father. Jesus told the disciples to remain in Jerusalem until endued with power from on high.

"But ye shall receive power, after that the Holy Ghost is come upon you..." (Acts 1:8).

Because of the Holy Spirit, we can say yes to the question, "can we know when the Rapture will occur?"

The events that unfold in the last days are known as the Day of the Lord. Many people misunderstand this period. Apostle Peter tried to clarify this by saying:

"But, beloved, be not ignorant of this one thing, that one day is with the Lord as a thousand years, and a thousand years as one day" (II Pe. 3:8).

The Day of the Lord can span thousands of years. We know that the Rapture DOESN'T happen at the beginning of the Day of the Lord because if it did, it would have happened on the Day of Pentecost. However, Peter said that the Day of Pentecost fulfilled what the prophet Joel spoke. Peter quotes Joel.

> *"But this is that which was spoken by the prophet Joel; And it shall come to pass in the last days, saith God, I will pour out of my Spirit upon all flesh: and your sons and your daughters shall prophesy, and your young men shall see visions, and your old men shall dream dreams: And on my servants and on my handmaidens I will pour out in those days of my Spirit; and they shall prophesy: And I will shew wonders in heaven above, and signs in the earth beneath; blood, and fire, and vapor of smoke: The sun shall be turned into darkness, and the moon into blood, before that great and notable day of the Lord come" (Acts 2:16-20).*

The first part has been fulfilled and is the start of the Day of the Lord. The latter part is happening thousands of years later. "And I will shew wonders in heaven above, and signs in the earth beneath; blood, and fire, and vapor of smoke: The sun shall be turned into darkness, and the moon into blood, before that great and notable day of the Lord come." So, the Rapture is in front of this happening. In other words, the Day of the Lord was triggered at the Day of Pentecost, but it isn't FULLY revealed until the Bride of Christ is snatched away and all the seals have been opened.

It is in these "times and seasons" that the cataclysmic events occur. The "new moon," or the moon turned into blood, is an indicator of this season. Paul said clearly that we as His Bride are not ignorant of the times and seasons; also, the moon indicates our seasons.

"He appointed the moon for seasons..." (Psa. 104:19).

One day we will see a "new moon," revealing the time and season of His return. There are four seasons a year. These seasons never change; they are a constant. We can look around and notice that the times in which we live are uncertain at best and very unusual. We are no longer living in "normal" times. The season He returns is connected to the feasts of God. The last three feasts have not been prophetically fulfilled. The next feast to be fulfilled is the "feast of trumpets." This feast ALWAYS occurs in the "fall" season. It would not be surprising that the last sound of the trumpets of Israel at the "feast of trumpets," will call His bride home. He is returning for His Bride. In the next Chapter, we will look at who His Bride is.

Chapter Four

The Bride of Christ

If a person tries to look it up in Strongs Concordance, they will not find the words "bride of Christ;" however, the word "bride" appears 14 times, and all of those times, it does not refer to an actual living person, and ALWAYS to someone in the future. Nine times she is spoken of in the book of Isaiah, Jeremiah, and Joel. Jesus refers to the name once, and John in the book of Revelation refers to her four times. Keep in mind that prophets of God speak of ALL the references.

> "...thou shalt surely clothe thee with them all, as with an ornament, and bind them on thee, as a bride doth" (Isa. 49:18).

> "...he hath covered me with the robe of righteousness, as a bridegroom decketh himself with ornaments, and as a bride adorneth herself with her jewels" (Isa. 60:10).

> "and as the Bridegroom rejoiceth over the Bride, so shall thy God rejoice over thee" (Isa. 62:5).

"Can a maid forget her ornaments, or a bride her attire? yet my people have forgotten me days without number" (Jer. 2:32).

"Then will I cause to cease from the cities of Judah, and from the streets of Jerusalem, the voice of mirth, and the voice of gladness, the voice of the Bridegroom, and the voice of the Bride: for the land shall be desolate" (Jer. 7:34).

"Behold, I will cause to cease out of this place in your eyes, and in your days, the voice of mirth, and the voice of gladness, the voice of the Bridegroom, and the voice of the Bride" (Jer. 16:9).

"Moreover I will take from them the voice of mirth, and the voice of gladness, the voice of the Bridegroom, and the voice of the Bride "(Jer. 25:10).

"The voice of joy, and the voice of gladness, the voice of the Bridegroom, and the voice of the Bride" (Jer. 33:11).

"let the Bridegroom go forth of His chamber, and the Bride out of her closet" (Joel 2:16).

"He that hath the Bride is the Bridegroom" (John 3:29).

"And the light of a candle shall shine no more at all in thee; and the voice of the Bridegroom and of the Bride shall be heard no more at all in thee" (Rev. 18:23).

"And I John saw the holy city, new Jerusalem, coming down from God out of heaven, prepared as a bride adorned for her husband" (Rev. 21:2).

"Come hither, I will shew thee the Bride, the Lamb's wife" (Rev. 21:9).

"And the Spirit and the Bride say, Come" (Rev. 22:17).

In the Old Testament, the Hebrew word, כַּלָּה (kal-law) is also interpreted as 'daughter-in-law' or 'spouse' (daughter-in-law [17x's], Bride [9x's], and spouse [8x's]. This word comes from the Hebrew root word, כָּלַל (kaw-lal'), which means 'completeness, or perfection.' It has different connotations in other languages in general; Biblical Aramaic and Syriac Shaph. שכלל, complete, finish; Assyrian kalâli III. I. 2. complete; Arabic is be wearied, fatigued; Aramaic כְּלִילָא, is a crown, hence denominative אֲכְלִיל, to crown; Ethiopic I. 2 to crown, a crown, crowning (of bride), nuptials; Arabic a crown. The complete idea is that this word gives us a picture of a crowned, perfected person, and this may be why He promised a crown for 'all those that love His appearing.' Who is the Bride? She is the perfected one crowned at the moment of His appearing.

In the Bible, we learn of specific conditions to be His Bride. First, she is redeemed. The Bride is dressed in white linen, speaking of Righteousness. It does not matter if a person has done great works in their life or attended religious services all their life; if they have not received Jesus Christ into their heart, having Him cleanse them of their sins with His redeeming blood, they can not be raptured. Second, they have to be ready. The Bible says, "his wife has made herself ready" (Rev. 19:7). What does this mean? It simply means that she is dressing up for the occasion. One has to be wearing a suitable garment (Mt. 22:11-13). This garment represents the "Righteousness of Jesus Christ." Any bride will prepare for her wedding day. She is expecting a wedding, prepared for the wedding, and is excited about this day. The second part of this verse is NOT complete without the first part. "Let us be glad and rejoice, and give honor to Him: for the marriage of the Lamb is come, and His wife hath made herself ready" (Rev. 19:7). This word, 'ready' comes from the idea of preparing a roadway so that it was passable by a King. It is the same word used by John the Baptist.

"The voice of him that crieth in the wilderness, 'Prepare' ye the way of the LORD, make straight in the desert a highway for our God" (Isa. 40:3).

The preparation is for Him, NOT for her. It was so He could see, not so she could. Everything is about Him, NOT her. Even the honor is given to Him, not to her. Usually, this is NOT the case at a wedding. The Bride is the focus; she is the one given that honor and attention. Even Apostle Peter told the husband to give the wife honor, lest his "prayers be hindered" (I Pe. 3:7).

The five foolish and the five wise virgins illustrate this truth. The cry to them all was to go to meet Him, but it was at night, so they needed to make sure that their lamps would NOT go out because otherwise, he would not have been able to see the roadway that He was traveling on. In this case, the ONLY difference between the wise and the foolish virgins was that the wise had what was necessary for the light to continue burning, thus the extra oil.

> *"Then shall the kingdom of heaven be likened unto ten virgins, which took their lamps, and went forth to meet the Bridegroom. And five of them were wise and five were foolish. They that were foolish took their lamps, and took no oil with them: But the wise took oil in their vessels with their lamps. While the Bridegroom tarried, they all slumbered and slept. And at midnight there was a cry made, Behold, the Bridegroom cometh; go ye out to meet him. Then all those virgins arose, and trimmed their lamps. And the foolish said unto the wise, Give us of your oil; for our lamps are gone out. But the wise answered, saying, Not so; lest there be not enough for us and you: but go ye rather to them that sell, and buy for yourselves. And while they went to buy the Bridegroom came; and they that were ready went in with him to the marriage: and the door was shut. Afterward came also the other virgins, saying, Lord, Lord, open to us. But he answered and said, Verily I say unto you, I know you not. Watch therefore, for ye know neither the day nor the hour wherein the Son of man cometh"* (Mt. 25:1-13).

The wise "took" oil in their vessel. This word, 'took' in this context, also means "accept" or "receive." It is an act of receiving or rejecting when taking it up. We receive the Holy Spirit, which is what the oil represents in this instance. Those vessels filled with the Holy Spirit need not be concerned about the light going out.

It would seem evident that the Church in Scripture is always referred to as a "she" and NOT a "he." We would expect this when it comes to His Church, but it is NOT so. In EVERY reference in the seven Churches of Asia, there is NO reference to "she." The ONLY reference to "she" is when "she" is seen as His Bride. The identifier here is the Bride, NOT the Church. There is a separation and a distinction. Just like when Jesus separated the "tares" and the "wheat." Consider the separation between the two wives of Abram, Naomi's two daughters-in-law (brides) in the book of Ruth, and two sets of virgins (wise and foolish).

Sarai (Sarah) and Hagar (Agar)

She is NOT of the flesh but the Spirit. There were two main wives of Abram. Sarai, and Hagar. Sarai gave Hagar to Abram so they would have children, but the promise was NOT to come forth from Hagar's womb but Sarah's. Apostle Paul opened up this allegory to us in the book of Galatians, referring to Hagar as of the flesh and Sarah as of the Spirit.

"For it is written, that Abraham had two sons, the one by a bondmaid, the other by a free woman. But he who was of the bondwoman was born after the flesh; but he of the free woman was by promise. Which things are an allegory: for these are the two covenants; the one from the mount Sinai, which genders to bondage, which is Agar. For this Agar is mount Sinai in Arabia, and answers to Jerusalem which now is, and is in bondage with her children. But Jerusalem which is above is free, which is the mother of us all...But as then he that was born after the flesh persecuted him that was born after the Spirit, even so it is now. Nevertheless what saith the Scripture? Cast out the bondwoman and her Son: for the Son of the bondwoman shall not be heir with the Son of the free woman. So then, brethren, we are not children of the bondwoman, but of the free" (Gal. 4:22-31).

Just as a bride receives a name change and shares in the name of her Bridegroom, a name change occurs in this instance. This name change for Sarai came AFTER Hagar was sent away, and the promised Son (Isaac) did not come out of the womb of Sarai (which womb was closed) but from the womb of Sarah. God changed her name from "princess" (Sarai) to 'noblewoman or "queen" (Sarah). The Bride of Christ is she that takes on a new name and receives her crown identifying her as His queen, because

He is the King of Kings, and NOW she as His Bride is a queen and is now called "Nobel" just like Sarah. We are kings and priests unto God and have taken on a nobility, sharing His name, just as Sarah now shares the name of God.

The Church of Philadelphia is given a new name. They are told they will escape the "hour of temptation" or trials (the Tribulation).

> *"Him that overcomes will I make a pillar in the temple of my God, and he shall go no more out: and I will write upon him the name of my God, and the name of the city of my God, which is new Jerusalem, which cometh down out of heaven from my God:* **and I will write upon him my new name**" *(Rev. 3:12).*

Note that the Churches are referred to in the "male" tense until the Church receives a new name, and afterward, we see the New Jerusalem as His Bride and is NOW a she, not he. We do NOT become the Bride of Christ unless we have this new name.

The Hebrew name YHWH (or Yahweh) has the letter "H" added to Sara(h), doing two things: sharing the name of God and replacing "I" with "H". So now we see the true meaning of being in Christ and the Christ-o-centric principle instead of the I-centric principle. There has to be a name change. The last consonant of the tetragram (Y-H-W-H) is also the last "universal key" of the name of God.

Philadelphia is the ONLY Church of the seven Churches of Asia, showing the "key of David" (NOT keys of David). According to Jewish writings, this is one of four universal keys (or from the four corners of the earth) taken from the very name of God Yahweh (יהוה)(Y-H-W-H). The fourth and "final" key is given to the Bride, and is referred to as "the key of David", or the "final key." (Soncino Zohar, Shemoth, Section 2, Page 133b-134b). The first three keys are united as ONE, according to Zech. 14:9, leaving the "final key" to be given to His Bride...and they shall be ONE flesh. Just as the promise of God came through Sarah, not Sarai, the promise of His appearing comes to the Bride and NOT the Church. The Jewish community would refer to this process as 'name immersion.' They also see this as the whole idea of redemption.

The Two Daughters-in-Law: Ruth and Orpah

The story of Ruth is another allegory that identifies us as the Bride of Christ. Boaz represented the Bridegroom, and Ruth represented the Bride of Christ. Orpah, the sister-in-law to Ruth, ultimately stayed in Moab, and Ruth came home with Naomi ending up in the City of Bethlehem, where she met Boaz, her soon-to-be husband. Jesus was born in Bethlehem. Just as Naomi and Ruth returned to the place where Jesus would one day appear, the Bride of Christ will one day return to the appearing of Jesus Christ and meet Him in the air.

The Shulamite Bride and the Daughters of Jerusalem

The Song of Solomon is another example of the Bride of Christ.

"I charge you, O daughters of Jerusalem, if ye find my beloved, that ye tell him, that I am sick of love. What is thy beloved more than another beloved, O thou fairest among women? What is thy beloved more than another beloved, that thou dost so charge us" (Song 5:8,9)?

Ishmael and Jerusalem's daughters mocked the promised Son (Gen. 21:8,9). Jesus, in His final hours, as a sacrificial lamb and being led to His crucifixion on the cross, identified the daughters of Jerusalem for who they were and where they would end up (in the Tribulation).

"But Jesus turning unto them said, Daughters of Jerusalem, weep not for me, but weep for yourselves, and for your children. For, behold the days are coming, in the which they shall say, Blessed are the barren, and the wombs that never bare, and the paps which never gave suck. Then shall they begin to say to the mountains, Fall on us; and to the hills, Cover us" (Lu. 23:28-30).

The very same thing was said of those in the book of Revelation.

"...And said to the mountains and rocks, Fall on us, and hide us from the face of Him that sitteth on the throne, and from the wrath of the Lamb: For the great day of His wrath is come; and who shall be able to stand" (Rev. 6:16,17)?

The book of the Song of Solomon compares the daughters of Jerusalem and the Shulamite maiden, who would one day be the queen. The difference was that they could not relate to the intimate way she described her lover, the Bridegroom (Song 5:10-16). How intimate was she?

"His mouth is most sweet: yea, he is altogether lovely. This is my beloved, and this is my friend, O daughters of Jerusalem" (Sng. 5:16).

It will not be a person's relationship to their Church that will make a difference, but their relationship to Jesus. How close are they to Jesus, and how close is He to them? She called Him her friend, and Jesus called His disciples' friends, who were once called "servants."

"Henceforth I call you not servants; for the servant knoweth not what his lord doeth: but I have called you

friends; for all things that I have heard of my Father I have made known unto you" (John 15:15).

The context of this verse is important. Jesus bookends this with the words, "love one another." It is not by accident that the writer of Hebrews says the same thing about the Rapture.

"And let us consider one another to provoke unto love and to good works: Not forsaking the assembling of ourselves together, as the manner of some is; but exhorting one another: and so much the more, as ye see the day approaching" (Heb. 10:24,25).

Those Who Do the Will of God and Those Who Do Not.

The Bride of Christ is not interested in impressing Jesus with what they have done.

"Not every one that saith unto me, Lord, Lord, shall enter into the kingdom of heaven; but he that doeth the will of my Father which is in heaven. Many will say to me in that day, Lord, Lord, have we not prophesied in thy name? and in thy name have cast out devils? and in thy name done many wonderful works? And then will I profess unto them, I never knew you: depart from me, ye that work iniquity" (Matt. 7:22,23).

It might be noted here that the word iniquity in Greek, ἀνομία (anomia), means "contempt for the law," which is the same word applied to the Antichrist.

"And then shall that Wicked (anomas) be revealed, whom the Lord shall consume with the spirit of his mouth, and shall destroy with the brightness of his coming" (II Thess. 2:8).

The Bible also uses the word "lawlessness" with how it affects our love relationships.

"And because iniquity (anomia) shall abound, the love of many shall wax cold" (Matt. 24:12).

The Bride of Christ is not lawless and loveless but lives out her life with the same delight as her Bridegroom.

"I delight to do thy will, O my God: yea, thy law is within my heart." (Psa. 40:8).

Jesus was fully aware of the works that the Churches did in Asia. In each of the seven Churches of Asia, he said, "I know thy works." We do not have to tell Him. He knows. What He is more interested in is our relationship with Him. In the next Chapter, we will see how Jesus discerns between them and which Church is 'rapture ready.'

❖

Chapter Five

The Seven Churches

Finally, how do we know there is a distinction between the Bride of Christ and others? To be clear, the Bride of Christ is the one He redeemed, but as His Bride, she must respond accordingly. Jesus shows his love by dying for her; ultimately, to be his Bride, she must love Him back. No bride becomes the Bride by saying NO to the groom. So the question is: will everyone who claims to be redeemed be raptured? If we look at the 7 Churches of Asia, we can tell that ALL Churches are NOT the same. Some of the Churches were NOT ready and were told that if they did not repent, they would go through the Tribulation. Therefore if they go through the Tribulation, they are not raptured and are not his Bride. Only the Bride is raptured because that is whom Jesus is meeting in the air. Jesus is NOT coming back for a church; He is coming back for a bride.

The Seven Churches of Asia

The seven Churches of Asia have often been used to show the timeline for when Jesus comes back. Ephesus was the first Church mentioned. Ephesus was, in reality, one of the first Churches historically. When the book of Revelation was written, there were hundreds of Churches. Why do we have only these Churches mentioned? One could suggest that John wanted to convey the significance of the "local church" because those mentioned were near the island of Patmos, where he was writing.

There may be a more simplistic reason for the "seven." Seven is the number for perfection and completeness. These Churches represent a "complete" picture of ALL Churches, past and present.

The Church of Philadelphia is the only Church with no concerns by our Lord. Could it be that these Churches were selected so that we would have a way of knowing "who" would be raptured and not "when?" Instead of a historical picture, we see a "comparative" one. The comparison of the Churches makes sense because of the order in which Jesus gave the Churches. Laodicea was the last Church mentioned. It is not likely that the Church He said He would spew out of His mouth would be His Bride.

Each of these Churches are given proclamations of being in the Tribulation or "kept" from it. All of the Churches listed were actual Churches that Jesus Himself identified and "stood in the midst" in Revelation Chapter One.

> *"And I turned to see the voice that spake with me. And being turned, I saw seven golden candlesticks; And in the midst of the seven candlesticks one like unto the Son of man, clothed with a garment down to the foot, and girt about the paps with a golden girdle...and the seven candlesticks which thou sawest are the seven churches"* (Rev. 1:12,13,20).

The Church of Ephesus

This Church is said to have "lost its first love." Also, if they did NOT repent, he would "remove" them from the standing Churches represented by the candlesticks where He stood in the midst. These two things would have disqualified the Church of Ephesus and would not have depicted His Bride.

The Church of Smyrna

> *"Fear none of those things which thou shalt suffer: behold, the devil shall cast some of you into prison, that ye may be tried; and ye shall have tribulation ten days: be thou faithful unto death, and I will give thee a crown of life"* (Rev. 2:10).

These could be those put to death because they refuse to worship the beast. They last ten days before this day comes. Jesus tells them to be 'faithful unto death to give them a "heads up" on what's to come.

The Church of Pergamum

Theologians know this Church as the compromising Church. Jesus told them that if they did not repent of the compromising ways, he would fight them with the sword of His mouth.

> *"Repent; or else I will come unto thee quickly, and will fight against them with the sword of my mouth" (Rev. 2:16).*

They went through the entire Tribulation up to the battle of Armageddon.

> *"And out of his mouth goeth a sharp sword, that with it he should smite the nations: and he shall rule them with a rod of iron: and he treadeth the winepress of the fierceness and wrath of Almighty God. And he hath on his vesture and on his thigh a name written, KING OF KINGS, AND LORD OF LORDS. And I saw an angel standing in the sun; and he cried with a loud voice, saying to all the fowls that fly in the midst of heaven,*

Come and gather yourselves together unto the supper of the great God" (Rev. 19:15-17).

If this is about the "battle of Armageddon," we know the Church of Pergamum would not have been part of the Bride of Christ because she comes with Him. She is not on the Earth, but is in the air.

The Church of Thyatira

"Behold, I will cast her into a bed, and them that commit adultery with her into GREAT TRIBULATION, except they repent of their deeds" (Rev. 2:22).

It is evident in this narrative that some were in this Church that did not follow in their wickedness.

"But unto you I say, and unto the rest in Thyatira, as many as have not this doctrine, and which have not known the depths of Satan, as they speak; I will put upon you none other burden" (Rev. 2:24).

The Church of Sardis

"Remember therefore how thou hast received and heard, and hold fast, and repent. If therefore thou shalt not watch, I will come on thee as a thief, and thou shalt not know what hour I will come upon thee" (Rev. 3:3).

In other passages of Scripture, Jesus speaks of coming as a thief in the night.

> "And this know, that if the goodman of the house had known what hour the thief would come, he would have watched, and not have suffered his house to be broken through. Be ye therefore ready also: for the Son of man cometh at an hour when ye think not. Then Peter said unto Him, Lord, speakest thou this parable unto us, or even to all? And the Lord said, Who then is that faithful and wise steward, whom his Lord shall make ruler over his household, to give them their portion of meat in due season? Blessed is that servant, whom his Lord when he cometh shall find so doing. Of a truth I say unto you, that he will make him ruler over all that he hath. But and if that servant say in his heart, My Lord delayeth his coming; and shall begin to beat the menservants and maidens, and to eat and drink, and to be drunken; The Lord of that servant will come in a day when he looketh not for him, and at an hour when he is not aware, and will cut him in sunder, and will appoint him his portion WITH THE UNBELIEVERS" (Lu. 12:39-46).

Jesus set forth this parable so that we would be ready for his return. Peter was confused about whom Jesus referred. Peter replied to Jesus: "is this to us or to all?" Jesus answered Peter, making it clear that he spoke of "believers" (faithful stewards) that acted like "unbelievers" and told Him that they would have their portion with the "unbelievers." Jesus later compared the five foolish and wise virgins in the same Gospel of Luke. They were all virgins and had lamps, but only five of the ten were ready when Jesus came back.

Paul also refers to the phrase "thief in the night." He distinguishes between the Church of Thessalonians and those in the "night."

> *"For yourselves know perfectly that the day of the Lord so cometh as a thief in the night" (I Thess. 5:2).*

The day of the Lord is not a foreign word in Scripture. The phrase "Day of the Lord" is also the day of indignation and the wrath of God. These words point to the beginnings of Tribulation, not the Rapture of the Church. The Bride of Christ is NOT caught off guard regarding the Rapture. When one reads this verse in context, they see two different kinds of people referenced—the Bride and the others, like the Church of Sardis.

> *"But of the times and the seasons, brethren, ye have no need that I write unto you. For yourselves know perfectly that the day of the Lord so cometh as a thief in the night. For when THEY shall say, Peace and safety; then sudden destruction cometh upon THEM, as travail upon a woman with child; and THEY shall not escape.*

> *But ye, brethren, are not in darkness, that that day should overtake you as a thief. Ye are all the children of light, and the children of the day: we are not of the night, nor of darkness" (I Thess. 5:1-5).*

There was a time when the times and the seasons could NOT be known. Jesus told his own disciples that.

> *"When they therefore were come together, they asked of Him, saying, Lord, wilt thou at this time restore again the kingdom to Israel? And he said unto them, It is not for you to know the times or the seasons, which the Father hath put in his own power. But ye shall receive power, after that the Holy Ghost is come upon you: and ye shall be witnesses unto me both in Jerusalem, and in all Judaea, and in Samaria, and unto the uttermost part of the earth" (Acts 1:6-8).*

The difference is that after they received power, they were given the ability to "know" the times and the seasons. Paul confirmed this when he told the Church of Thessalonians that they knew the times and the seasons. It makes sense that the difference between the time before the Holy Spirit came on the day of Pentecost and the time afterward is that NOW we are in the dispensation of the Holy Spirit. He has granted us the power to know something that could NOT be known without the Holy Spirit. We need the Holy Spirit in our lives because He leads us into all truth. Just as the wise virgins had "enough" oil to "go out to meet him" we need to have enough Holy Spirit to be ready to meet Him in the air when he returns. One could say that the Holy Spirit is that rocket fuel needed to make the journey upward when the trumpet sounds. The admonition in Scripture is clear…" be FILLED with the Spirit."

> *"But all things that are reproved are made manifest by the light: for whatsoever doth make manifest is light. Wherefore he saith, Awake thou that sleepest, and arise from the dead, and Christ shall give thee light. See then that ye walk circumspectly, not as fools, but as wise, Redeeming the time, because the days are evil. Wherefore be ye not unwise, but understanding what the will of the Lord is. And be not drunk with wine, wherein is excess; but be filled with the Spirit" (Eph. 5:13-18).*

A person would have thought that Paul had just read about the five foolish and the five wise virgins. This message of Paul would have served the Church of Sardis well. They were known as the 'dead' Church, which Paul said to 'arise from the dead, and Christ shall give thee light." The five foolish did NOT have what it took to sustain the light because they were NOT filled with the Spirit. The Baptism of the Holy Spirit was a command spoken by both Jesus and Paul. It was an imperative.

Following this command, Paul speaks of how to be filled with the Spirit. He follows with participles (which are NOT commands).

1. "Speaking to yourselves in psalms and hymns and spiritual songs, singing and making melody in your heart to the Lord;
2. Giving thanks always for all things unto God and the Father in the name of our Lord Jesus Christ;
3. Submitting yourselves one to another in the fear of God" (Eph. 5:19-21).

One could say that these three things the five foolish virgins lacked and the five wise virgins possessed. Paul began with the words,

> "See then that ye walk circumspectly, not as fools, but as wise, Redeeming the time, because the days are evil" (Eph. 5:15,16).

Remember that the advice given to the foolish virgins (those that were NOT wise) was advised to go and 'buy' from the merchants that sell. The word "buy" is the same word "redeem," which means "to make one's own." They should have "redeemed the time," knowing the days were evil, but they waited until later.

One can also see this SAME admonition given in Colossians 3, which has to do with the Rapture because he says so in this Chapter.

> "When Christ, who is our life, shall appear, then shall ye also appear with Him in glory" (Col. 3:4).

The Church of Philadelphia

The Church of Philadelphia is the ONLY Church that is not told to repent; it is the ONLY Church that receives a NEW NAME (Name Change); it is the ONLY Church shown an open door (the same as John who was caught up to heaven in Chapter four of Revelation), Jesus told this Church:

> "Behold, I have set before thee an open door" (Rev. 3:8);

The Church of Philadelpia is the ONLY Church given the "final" key, called the "key of David," given to the Bride. This is NOT referring to the "keys of David" in the Old Testament. This is notably the "key of David," which is special and unique. This Church is kept from the Tribulation because she is raptured. She resembles the Bride of Christ. The language used is bridal, and the promise to "keep her from the hour of temptation" is given. This promise is NOT to any of the other Churches.

Historically, Philadelphia was a region that experienced many earthquakes. When they came, the people would immediately proceed out of the City to protect themselves from falling buildings and debris. Jesus promised them that a day would come that this overcoming Church would "go no more out" (Rev. 3:12). When the sixth seal is opened, an earthquake occurs.

"And I beheld when he had opened the sixth seal, and, lo, there was a great earthquake..." (Rev. 6:12).

Jesus was able to promise this Church that they would "go no more out" because they would be going up, not out. The earthquake would NOT harm them because he would be snatching them away at that very moment.

Jesus identifies this Church with the New Jerusalem, which we learn later is the Bride of Christ.

"...and I will write upon him the name of my God, and the name of the city of my God, which is new Jerusalem, which cometh down out of heaven from my God: and I will write upon him my new name" (Rev. 3:12).

Later in the book of Revelation, John calls the City that descends from heaven as the New Jerusalem, the Bride of Christ.

> "And I John saw the holy city, New Jerusalem, coming down from God out of heaven, prepared as a bride adorned for her husband" (Rev. 21:2).

The Church of Laodicea

This Church is said to be Luke warm, and as such, He would spew them out of his mouth.

> *So then because thou art lukewarm, and neither cold nor hot, I will spue thee out of my mouth"* (Rev. 3:16).

He refers to this Church as 'wretched, and miserable, and poor, and blind, and naked". Certainly NOT describing what a bride would look like. In contrast, Jesus gives them counsel to BE what a Bride would look like:

> *"I counsel thee to buy of me gold tried in the fire, that thou mayest be rich; and white raiment, that thou mayest be clothed, and that the shame of thy nakedness do not appear; and anoint thine eyes with eyesalve, that thou mayest see"* (Rev. 3:18).

The Bride is NOT poor and will be in a white wedding dress because she is clothed in His Righteousness.

The Bridegroom was seen in the midst of the Churches. The idea that a person does not need to be in a local Church is misleading and even deceptive. The Bride of

Christ was among the candlesticks, not apart from them. She was counted as one of them, not separate from them. Some Christians see the need to separate themselves from others in an attempt to be more holy or spiritual. This is not the attitude or Spirit of His Bride. The Bride of Christ is not Aloof or distant and unfriendly towards other Christians, but they are brotherly. Paul admonishes those who are strong spiritually to be supportive of those who are not. A person needs to be with people to accomplish this.

"We then that are strong ought to bear the infirmities of the weak, and not to please ourselves" (Ro. 15:1).

The Bride of Christ is one of these seven Churches. The most likely one is the Church of Philadelphia. All the other Churches were given grave instructions or else. This Church was admonished to keep going strong and given promises for doing so. They were told to hold fast to what they had and let no one take their crown. This crown was given to all those that love His appearing.

Looking at the Bride, we can best see the Church that is NOT his Bride. Paul specified two groups of people to be raptured: the dead in Christ and those still alive and remained on the earth at his coming.

"For the Lord Himself shall descend from heaven with a shout, with the voice of the archangel, and with the

trump of God: and the dead in Christ shall rise first: Then we which are alive and remain shall be caught up together with them in the clouds, to meet the Lord in the air: and so shall we ever be with the Lord" (I Thess. 4:16,17).

First, the dead in Christ rise first. The Rapture of His Bride is NOT escapism but an intimate event. The dead have nothing to escape from. They are dead. Jesus is coming back for a Bride.

In Christ

The Bride of Christ is "in Christ." In Christ is an essential doctrine. It is known among theologians as the "Christ-o-centric principle." The early Christians were not called Christians because they were religious. Remember, they were not first called Christians in Jerusalem, but they were first called Christians in Antioch. Jerusalem was the religious headquarters of the Apostles of Christ, yet it was not until they were in Antioch that they were called Christians. Why? It was not until they lived out their faith that people recognized that they were "Christ ones" and were distinct from the religious community. Being in Christ means a change occurs.

"Therefore if any man be in Christ, he is a new creature: old things are passed away; behold, all things are become new" (II Cor. 5:17).

Paul made it a point to identify himself as "in Christ" when he was "caught up."

"I knew a man in Christ above fourteen years ago, (whether in the body, I cannot tell; or whether out of the body, I cannot tell: God knoweth;) such an one caught up to the third heaven" (II Cor. 12:2).

What it looks like to be in Christ is illustrated in the book of Ephesians. He speaks of this also concerning the Rapture.

"That in the dispensation of the fulness of times he might gather together in one all things in Christ, both which are in heaven, and which are on earth; even in Him" (Eph. 1:10).

When a person reads Ephesians, there is no guessing what is meant to be in Christ.

"For we are his workmanship, created in Christ Jesus unto good works, which God hath before ordained that we should walk in them" (Eph. 2:10).

This is why several New Testament authors, including Jesus Himself, gave a list of things to forsake and live differently.

"In Him we live, and move, and have our being" (Acts 17:28).

Babylon, the Great Whore

"And the light of a candle shall shine no more at all in thee; and the voice of the Bridegroom and of the Bride shall be heard no more at all in thee: for thy merchants were the great men of the earth; for by thy sorceries were all nations deceived. And in her was found the blood of prophets, saints, and all that were slain upon the earth" (Rev. 18:23,24).

This character in the book of Revelation is said to be a mystery. She rides on the beast and seems to have political influence in the world. We see her as one that is AGAINST the true saints of God. In this verse, she is seen as one that light is taken from; the Bridegroom's voice and the Bride are no longer heard. She has some kind of religious connection. Remember, Jesus told His disciples that they were the world's light. Jesus said that unless the light is on a candlestick, it is hid. Here we find that with Babylon, it is no more. The one who produces the light is gone. Babylon is living in the time of the Antichrist, and she is "riding" on the beast. The Bride is GONE. This is why her voice is no longer heard.

Some people believe that due to the colors describing her, she is representative of the Catholic Church. Since the Catholic Church has such a global influence on people and governments around the world and has a great influence on the leaders of the world, this could be an accurate depiction. There are certainly those that are of His Bride among the Catholic Church. I know plenty. Here we find that their voice is no longer heard in this instance. Why? Because they are no longer there. This is another example of the Bride of Christ missing during the Tribulation. The religions of the world are still there, but NOT his Bride.

We know that this is NOT an actual person, like the Pope or other world leaders, because she is NOT thrown into the lake of fire. In the end the Devil, the Antichrist, and the false prophet are thrown into the lake of fire, but NOT the Great Whore, mystery Babylon. This is because she is NOT a person of interest, but instead, a powerful, religious system. It could be said of her that she is an ante-type of the true Church, which is called the City of our Great God, the New Jerusalem. Babylon is also referred to as a Great City, but not of God, but of the Devil. She is riding on the beast. She is also called a fornicator with the world's leaders, meaning that as a spiritual fornicator, she would be equivalent to Esau, who should have been God's firstborn but GAVE UP his birthright. She should have been more, she was adorned in beauty, and on the outward appearance, she was something to be amazed by, but inwardly she was wicked. Fornication in the Bible has to do with many things that have to do with immorality and idolatry. It also conveys 'unlawful' intimacy. The Bride of Christ is not so but is found in the union of Holy Matrimony. She was an adulterer. There was no union or covenant with Christ, just the appearance and nothing more. Paul speaks of this.

> "This know also, that in the last days perilous times shall come. For men shall be lovers of their own selves, covetous, boasters, proud, blasphemers, disobedient to parents, unthankful, unholy, Without natural affection, trucebreakers, false accusers, incontinent, fierce, despisers of those that are good, Traitors, heady, highminded, lovers of pleasures more than lovers of God; Having a form of godliness, but denying the power thereof: from such turn away" (II Tim. 3:1-5).

The clue to this verse is found in the beginning words, 'men shall be lovers of their selves.' Instead of loving others, they are consumed with loving themselves. Instead of being focussed on Christ, they are focussed on themselves. The Bride of Christ is NOT selfish.

Chapter Six

The First Five Seals

At the time of the opening of the sixth seal, the Day of the Lord is declared as 'fully' come, or also known as the "great day of his wrath." This day continues until the completion of the opening of the seventh seal.

Before the sixth seal is opened, five prior seals have been opened. The first four are in the appearance of the 4 horsemen. Jesus gives reference to these events by saying that these are the "beginning of sorrows" (Matt. 24:8). We may have had a taste of the fourth horseman through the plagues known as the Corona viruses, and it appears that they have not finished their ride. There is much speculation as to what these seals mean in today's world. If we follow the horses through the words of Christ in Matthew 24 we would see the seals interpreted in the following manner:

1st Seal (Deception—the White Horse)

"And Jesus answered and said unto them, Take heed that no man deceive you. For many shall come in my name, saying, I am Christ; and shall deceive many" (Matt. 24:4,5).

Some believe that this horse represents the Antichrist. This author does not. This author believes that this is NOT the Antichrist is because AFTER Jesus mentions deception in verse 4, he closely matches the rest of the horses with His words. The Antichrist is NOT mentioned until AFTER this list which He identifies as the "beginning of sorrows." Also, John does not speak of the Antichrist until After these seals are opened, including the sixth seal. The Antichrist or the Beast is NOT introduced until chapter 13. Jesus does, however, warn of deception. This is likely the meaning of this white horse.

The other thought about deception concerns a person, NOT just a teaching. They would come and try to appear as if they were Jesus Christ.

All the other horse riders are NOT people, so as these horsemen have commonality, this horseman would NOT be a person, matching all the other horse riders.

2nd Seal (Wars—the Red Horse)

> "And ye shall hear of wars and rumors of wars: see that ye be not troubled: for all these things must come to pass, but the end is not yet" (Matt. 24:6).

The author finds it interesting that the color used for the second seal is 'red' and the color that communism uses is also "red." This regime has been responsible for more wars than any other. Russia currently has red as its color. "Red" China is proudly shown as their color. Nazism, under the dictatorship of Adolf Hitler, was birthed out of communism. At that time, communism was the "workers' party." The Nazi swastika logo is black and "red." Red is the color of blood. War ALWAYS causes bloodshed. It is an appropriate color to represent war. As of this writing, Russia is causing much bloodshed in Ukraine. The prophetic significance of this atrocity is that the Bible indicates a "bear" coming down from the North and eventually attacking Israel, God's people.

3rd Seal (Poverty and Racial Unrest—the Black Horse)

> "For nation shall rise against nation, and kingdom against kingdom, and there shall be famines…" (Matt. 24:7).

The Greek word for nation is "ethnos" or "race." The word "rise up" in the original Greek refers to something that has already occurred but is "resurrected" afresh. These horses continue to ride. This black horse indicates many things; some are more obvious than others. The scales are not one but two, and the message is injustice and economic decline resulting in food shortages and famine. We are seeing this in vivid color today.

4th Seal (Universal Death—the Pale Horse)

"and pestilences…" (Matt. 24:7)

This seal is more prominent now than it ever was. Since 2020 and the release of the deadly virus known as the Corona Virus, we have a clearer idea of how many people can die around the world. This seal reveals death on the earth; just as this virus is global, this seal is global. This fourth seal reveals the combination of deaths that the red and black horses bring.

These first seals are together in purpose, which is why they are ALL seen as horses riding. This author believes they ride collectively and NOT just consecutively.

"All these are the beginning of sorrows" (Matt. 24:8).

5th Seal (the Completion of the Martyr's Vengeance)

> "When He opened the fifth seal, I saw under the altar the souls of those who had been slain for the word of God and for the testimony which they held. And they cried with a loud voice, saying, How long, O Lord, holy and true, until You judge and avenge our blood on those who dwell on the earth" (Rev. 6:9-10).

Who are these "slain souls?" Some might say they are the Raptured Church, but this is NOT what it says here. He says, "who had been slain for the word of God and the testimony which they held." If this were true, the Raptured Church would have had to die or be martyred to qualify. This seal addresses all who died after Pentecost for the witness they held. Note what Jesus said about these who would be martyred:

> "But ye shall receive power, after that the Holy Ghost is come upon you: and ye shall be witnesses unto me both in Jerusalem, and in all Judaea, and in Samaria, and unto the uttermost part of the earth" (Acts 1:8).

The word "witnesses" here is the Greek word, μάρτυρες (martures), from which we get the word martyr.

If one takes all the souls martyred from Abel (the first Martyr) to the opening of this seal, this would be them. Why were they found "under" the altar?

This altar would have to be the altar of sacrifice. These souls were slain as if they were nothing more than a piece of meat. However, God sees them as sweet-smelling savors. He sees it as an offering of themselves to God. The cry of the slain soul is ALWAYS heard. Note what God told Cain after he murdered Abel. "And he said, What hast thou done? the voice of thy brother's **blood** cries unto me from the ground" (Gen. 4:10).

The Importance of the Fifth Seal and Martyred Souls

The ceremony of blood that was taken from the sacrifice at the altar was walked into the presence of God and sprinkled on the Mercy seat. Bringing this blood to the Mercy Seat completed redemption. Remember, without the shedding of blood, there is no remission for sin or redemption.

> *"That upon you may come all the righteous blood shed upon the earth, from the blood of righteous Abel unto the blood of Zachariah son of Barachias, whom ye slew between the temple and the altar" (Matt. 23:35).*

This seal fulfilled those martyred from Abel (the first Martyr) to Zechariah (the last Martyr) in the Old Testament. Now, here we have the martyrs honored from the first Martyr AFTER Pentecost to the last Martyr before their blood is gathered to sprinkle in the Holy Place so that the seals can continue to open. One could say that as far as the Tribulation is concerned, this seal is the beginning of the end.

Notice what the author says in the book of Hebrews:

"And to Jesus the mediator of the new covenant, and to the blood of sprinkling, that speaks better things than that of Abel. See that ye refuse not Him that speaks. For if they escaped not who refused Him that spoke on earth, much more shall not we escape, if we turn away from Him that speaks from heaven: Whose voice then shook the earth: but now he hath promised, saying, Yet once more I shake not the earth only, but also heaven" (Heb. 12:24-26).

Could the author of Hebrews be alluding to the same event that Apostle John speaks of? Trumpets were blown, becoming louder with each blast. An earthquake occurred. We know that at the 'last trump' we shall be caught up, and according to John, an earthquake will happen, and the heavens shake.

The celebration of Pentecost also included this moment of commemorating the giving of the Law. Following this particular feast is the feast of trumpets just as the Rapture is the very next event in God's prophetic timeline following the day of Pentecost.

It is NOT by accident that Apostle Paul identifies the Antichrist as the "lawless" one who appears AFTER the restrainer is taken away (II Thess. 2:8). Notice the last part of Hebrews 12:26: "but now he hath promised, saying, Yet once more I shake not the earth ONLY, but also heaven." What is he referring to? This could be the EXACT moment He is referring to because what follows when blood is spilled: the earth shakes and the heavens darken. Note:

> *"Jesus, when he had cried again with a loud voice, yielded up the ghost. And, behold, the veil of the temple was rent in twain from the top to the bottom; and the earth did quake, and the rocks rent; And the graves were opened; and many bodies of the saints which slept arose, And came out of the graves after his resurrection, and went into the holy city, and appeared unto many" (Matt. 27:50-53; Mk. 15:33).*

When Jesus' blood spilled out, the earth shook, the sky became darkened, and the Sun was "darkened" (Lu. 23:45). Following that people were resurrected from the graves. The pattern has already been seen in the life of Jesus Christ.

Here the slain saints cry out LOUDLY for vengeance, their innocent shed blood is declared, the earth is shaken and the saints of God arise. Just like it happened at Jesus' death.

Let us look at what Isaiah the prophet said about this time:

> "Like as a woman with child, that draweth near the time of her delivery, is in pain, and crieth out in her pangs; so have we been in thy sight, O LORD. We have been with child, we have been in pain, we have as it were brought forth wind; we have not wrought any deliverance in the earth; neither have the inhabitants of the world fallen" (Isa. 26:17-18).

Jesus, in Matthew 24 said that the things described by Him and also repeated in the vision of John with the four horsemen were the beginning of "sorrows" (Matt. 24:8) or in the Greek "**the pain of childbirth, travail pain, birth pangs.**" (STRONGS). Here, Isaiah speaks first of birthing pains and then proceeds to describe what appears to be a description of the Rapture of His Bride.

> "Your dead shall live; Together with my dead body they shall arise. Awake and sing, you who dwell in dust; For your dew is like the dew of herbs, And the earth shall cast out the dead. Come, my people, enter thou into thy chambers, and shut thy doors about thee: hide thyself as it were for a little moment, until the indignation be over past. For, behold, the LORD cometh out of his place to punish the inhabitants of the earth for their iniquity: the earth also shall disclose her blood, and shall no more cover her slain" (Isa. 26:19-21).

"Enter into thy chambers" speaks of the Bride of Christ meeting with the Bridegroom to consummate the marriage. "The earth also shall disclose her blood and shall no more cover her slain" speaks of this very moment where those martyrs hidden under the altar will no longer be covered but shall be "disclosed." At the time of Jesus' crucifixion, an earthquake followed the "spilling" of blood. The sixth seal is opened at this very moment, and the Bride goes up.

Also, remember that there are no chapters in the original Hebrew language, so Chapter 26 continues into Chapter 27. Notice what day Isaiah is referring to:

"In that day the LORD with his sore and great and strong sword shall punish leviathan the piercing serpent, even leviathan that crooked serpent; and he shall slay the dragon that is in the sea" (Isa. 27:1).

The Beast (or the Antichrist) comes from the sea, and the Devil is called the dragon in Revelation chapter thirteen.

*"And I stood upon the sand of the sea, and saw a beast **rise up out of the sea**, having seven heads and ten horns, and upon his horns ten crowns, and upon his heads the name of blasphemy. And the Beast which I saw was like unto a leopard, and his feet were as the feet of a bear, and his mouth as the mouth of a*

lion: **and the dragon** gave him his power, and his seat, and great authority" (Rev. 13:1-3).

We also see the Beast wounded by a sword:

*"that they should make an image to the beast, which had the wound **by a sword**, and did live" (Rev. 13:14).*

So this fits the timeline here in Revelation 6:12 and what Isaiah saw in Isaiah 26 and 27. AFTER the Rapture, the Tribulation begins, the Beast appears, The Lord wounds him with a sword, as Isaiah records it in Chapter 27 of Isaiah.

The fifth seal is complete when they receive their white robes.

"Then a white robe was given to each of them; and it was said to them that they should rest a little while longer, until both the number of their fellow servants and their brethren, who would be killed as they were, was completed" (Rev. 6:11).

They received a white robe because they were pure before God. Sometimes when we go through persecution, we can doubt our purity and perhaps feel we deserve it. God gave them white to wear to show that they were pure before God and He wanted the whole world to know.

These Martyrs were told to pause and rest a while longer. Why? Just like the last Martyr had to be counted in the Old Testament, the last Martyr had NOT been counted in the New Testament. "until both the number of their fellow servants AND their brethren, who would be killed as they were, was completed." Then and only then could there be a complete blood offering, finishing redemption and calling the Bride of Christ home. We do NOT see ANYONE repenting or asking for Salvation AFTER this point in the book of Revelation.

So when it comes to the fifth seal, we see several scriptures illustrating the importance of the blood sacrifice.

Without the shedding of blood, there is no remission for sin. There is NO redemption. God told Cain in the book of Genesis: "the voice of thy brother's blood crieth unto me from the ground" (Gen. 4:10).

> "And they cried with a loud voice, saying, How long, O Lord, holy and true, dost thou not judge and avenge our blood on them that dwell on the earth" (Rev. 6:10).

Chapter Seven

The Opening of the Sixth Seal

This is the 'times and the seasons' when the Rapture occurs. It is here where the language used gives us meaningful revelation concerning the timing AND the event itself. Sometimes God will give you a clue about a scripture by using a certain word or words to introduce the verse. For instance Jesus would often start what he was saying with "verily, verily." He didn't do that for no reason. He wanted you to take notice to what he was about to say. He also wanted you to know that what he was going to say was important to listen to. In those words alone there is a sermon. It is no different when introducing words with the word, "behold." This word has deep meaning and it is used several times to introduce the coming of the Lord. Both Apostles John and Paul use this word. John actually uses it twice. In this instance He is 'sandwiching' the opening of the seal with this word.

> "And I beheld (ἰδού) when he had opened the sixth seal, and, lo (ἰδού)..." (Rev. 6:12).

This word is used elsewhere in Scripture to introduce us to what is known as the Rapture of the Church. Apostle Paul uses the exact same word to introduce to us this mystery.

> "Behold (ἰδού), I shew you a mystery; We shall not all sleep, but we shall all be changed, In a moment, in the twinkling of an eye, at the last trump: for the trumpet shall sound, and the dead shall be raised incorruptible, and we shall be changed" (I Cor. 15:51,52).

When Jesus is addressing the Church of Philadelphia, He uses this both in setting the open door before it, and the deliverance from the Tribulation period. In His explanation of 'keeping them from the hour of temptation Jesus uses this word twice, which also is 'sandwiching' the event of delivering them from the Tribulation. This is NOT a coincidence. It is quite on purpose. They both have something to do with each other. He is drawing our attention to this event by not only using the word, but using it in the exact same way. You might miss it if using the word once; but twice?

> "I know thy works: behold (ἰδού), I have set before thee an open door...Because thou hast kept the word

of my patience, I also will keep thee from the hour of temptation, which shall come upon all the world, to try them that dwell upon the earth. Behold (ἰδού), I come quickly" (Rev. 3:8,10,11).

Jesus also used this word when speaking about the bridegroom coming for His bride in the parable of the five wise and foolish virgins.

"And at midnight there was a cry made, behold (ἰδού), the bridegroom cometh; go ye out to meet him" (Matt. 25:6).

Sometimes in Scripture we are given a 'heads-up' which we should pay attention to. I believe that this is that 'heads-up' that our Lord spoke to his disciples about this moment in time.

John is NOT the first to speak of these cataclysmic events AND allude to His coming. John chooses to use figurative language and the use of certain Greek words to convey the idea of the Rapture. But Jesus ties BOTH cataclysmic events AND His coming together. This way there is NO doubt what is happening.

"And there shall be signs in the sun, and in the moon, and in the stars…And then shall they see the Son of man coming in a cloud with power and great glory. And when these things begin to come to pass, then look up,

and lift up your heads; for your redemption draweth nigh" (Lu. 21:25,27,28).

Naturally, we will be looking up when these cataclysmic events unfold; and as they unfold, we will see Him in the clouds and hear the trump sound and hear his voice say, "come-up." These events will be his calling card. The 'beginning of sorrows will be past, the fifth seal will have been opened, and the sixth seal will open with the heavens shaken, and simultaneously his bride will meet Him in the clouds and taken into his chamber and the door will be shut.

This was prophesied by Isaiah long before Jesus spoke similar words in a parable concerning the bride of Christ. Notice that both Isaiah AND Jesus make mention of the 'door' being closed. What door is He talking about? Could this be the same door that was open to the Church of Philadelphia and the open door that John saw before he was taken up?

"...behold, I have set before thee an open door" (Rev. 3:8).

"...and behold, a door was opened in heaven: and the first voice which I heard was as it were of a trumpet talking with me: which said, come up hither..."(Rev. 4:1).

*"Come, my people, enter thou into thy chambers, **and shut thy doors about thee**: hide thyself as it were for a little moment, until the indignation be over past"* (Isa. 26:20).

*"Then shall the kingdom of heaven be likened unto ten virgins, which took their lamps, and went forth to meet the bridegroom...And while they went to buy, the bridegroom came; and they that were ready went in with him to the marriage: **and the door was shut**. Afterward came also the other virgins, saying, Lord, Lord, open to us. But he answered and said, Verily I say unto you, I know you not. Watch therefore, for ye know neither the day nor the hour wherein the Son of man cometh" (Matt. 24:1-13).*

The following chapters we are going to be looking at certain words that are used to illustrate this wondrous event called the Rapture of His bride. These words punctuate this truth behind the scenes that follow. They are important words and when understood Biblically the mystery that Paul speaks of (I Cor. 15:51) concerning the Rapture of the Church can be seen.

To some people these words will be meaningless and they will be shrugged off as language used to describe to the best of John's knowledge of these cataclysmic events and nothing more. I disagree. In Scripture, words mean things, and they can have meaning within themselves.

Jesus taught this principle when he spoke parables. The story itself was not the end in itself, but had a purpose or meaning behind the story. He told them that ONLY those who it was to be given would understand.

Figurative language can be tricky. When you combine that with something that is LITERALLY going to happen it becomes even more of a challenge. This is where it is critical to be guided by the rules of hermeneutics to come up with its meaning. Allowing other scriptures to interpret Scripture is very useful in digging out the treasures that are there. David cried out a prayer that I hope is your desire as well. I know it is mine.

> *"Open thou mine eyes, that I may behold wondrous things out of thy law" (Psa. 119:18).*

Another thing that is important is looking at patterns. God is a pattern maker. He gave a pattern to Noah so he could build an ark. God gave Moses a pattern so that he would have a proper tabernacle. Nothing was left to chance. Each of these patterns were for the sake of revealing Christ. The pattern was also given to show that God ALWAYS gives his people an idea of what is in His mind before He reveals it later. The articles of the tabernacle were in the shape of a cross, which was the foretelling of what was to come. Patterns have a way of doing that.

It is no different with the Rapture. He gives us the pattern for this when Jesus died on the cross. Jesus shed his blood, the fifth seal of Revelation is the revealing of blood. After the shedding of blood came an earthquake; both at Calvary and here in the opening of the sixth seal. After the earthquake came the opening of the graves of many people. After the earthquake will come the Rapture which we know the dead in Christ will rise first. So the pattern is:

1. The blood
2. The earthquake
3. The graves open

This is the pattern repeated, seen here in Revelation 6:11,12).

The opening of the sixth seal is the beginning of the Tribulation and also the snatching away of his bride. After these events unfold those on the earth respond with these words:

"For the great day of his wrath is come; and who shall be able to stand" (Rev. 6:17).

Later, John sees a multitude that is identified as a people that come out of great tribulation.

> "And one of the elders answered, saying unto me, What are these which are arrayed in white robes? and whence came they? And I said unto him, Sir, thou knowest. And he said to me, These are they which came out of great tribulation" (Rev. 7:13,14).

According to Strongs Concordance these words 'out of' is actually one word, ἐξ, which means: "out of, from, by, away from." So this multitude which is later seen is literally taken "away from" the Tribulation or "out of" the Tribulation. This word, ἐξ is where we have the word Exodus. In the same sense as when God snatched Israel out of Egypt He is using this same word here to illustrate the snatching away of His people. This is where types and shadows appear in the OT so that we can be sure of it now. "In the mouth of two or three witnesses let every word be established" (Mt. 18:16). We see similitudes throughout the Scriptures. When Abraham was told to sacrifice his ONLY begotten son on mount Moriah, which later in Scripture we find God's only Son sacrificed on this same mountain thousands of years later. There are numerous passages of Scripture where we can draw 'confirmations' of things said in the Old Testament concerning the times in which we live.

Current events alone do NOT give us this confirmation, but the Scriptures do. In the days of Adolf Hitler, the Church was convinced that the time of the end had come, and the Antichrist had appeared. Although he was evil, he was NOT the Antichrist. Current events can come and go, but the one thing that is certain is the Word of God.

In the midst of Jesus' reply to his disciples about the end times he spoke these words:

"Heaven and earth shall pass away, but my words shall not pass away" (Mt. 24:35).

Following these words Jesus said, "But of that day and hour knoweth no man, no, not the angels of heaven, but my Father only" (Mt. 24:36).

Why? He wanted us to know that the ONLY thing we can be sure of is the Word of God. This is why we need to give heed to the Scriptures and why we need to seek out the Word of God when it comes to the study of end times. Jesus is giving us a key to understanding end times. The Scriptures alone are the key to unlocking the mysteries of the Bible. Paul said regarding this event of the Rapture, that it was a mystery. There is no better way of understanding mysteries than through the Scriptures. Jesus told the Sadducees that

"...you do err not knowing the Scriptures..." (Mt. 22:29).

This was said concerning the resurrection, which is EXACTLY what the Rapture resembles. It is not a coincidence that Apostle Paul used the entire Chapter 15 of I Corinthians to speak of the resurrection of the dead. The Chapter is divided up into three sections:

1. The fact of the Resurrection (vs. 1-19).
2. The order of the Resurrection (vs. 20-49).
3. The Mystery of the Resurrection (vs. 50-58).

The study of the Rapture has everything to do with the study of the resurrection. Paul is stating if the resurrection of Christ happened, and it happened in a certain order, then why is it difficult to believe that it will happen again with the Rapture?

Another thing we see in the opening of the sixth seal is that the scroll is NOW open. The way the seals were placed was as the information in the seal was read the scroll would continue to open until the next seal. Gradually the seals would be pealed away inside the scroll until all of the seals were opened and the scroll had been completely read. At this time the scroll had been opened with only the last seal to remain. The sixth seal opens the scroll to where we begin the Tribulation period. Isaiah recognizes this when he reiterates this event that John speaks of but also mentions the scroll.

"And all the host of heaven shall be dissolved, and the heavens shall be rolled together as a scroll" (Isa. 34:4).

The scroll is open already when the sixth seal is opened. If you continue the verse in Isaiah it reads:

"...and all their host shall fall down, as the leaf falleth off from the vine, and as a falling fig from the fig tree" (Isa. 34:4).

Apostle John gives similar words:

"And the stars of heaven fell unto the earth, even as a fig tree casteth her untimely figs, when she is shaken of a mighty wind" (Rev. 6:12).

In the following chapter we will look into the meaning of the word, "fig," and how it fits into the Rapture of His Bride.

Chapter Eight

Words Revealing the Rapture

In the cataclysmic events, John uses words that reveal a picture of more than just the events themselves. We can see this coded (Rev. 1:2) language revealed. It is helpful to examine these words to understand this truth. The theme in all this is the Rapture of His Bride. As we look at these words, we can see shreds of evidence of this, and we should embrace them.

The Earthquake

> *"And I beheld when he had opened the sixth seal, and, lo, there was a great earthquake" (Rev. 6:12).*

As noted earlier, there was a promise to the Church of Philadelphia that they "would go no more out" (Rev. 3:12). Philadelphia was known for earthquakes. When they occurred, the people would run out of the city to be safe from falling buildings. The remnants of the pillars are still a reminder of the promise God gave them.

> *"Him that overcomes will I make a pillar in the temple of my God, and he shall 'go no more out': and I will write upon him the name of my God, and the name of the city of my God, which is new Jerusalem, which comes down out of Heaven from my God: and I will write upon him my new name" (Rev. 3:12).*

The new Jerusalem is later called the "Bride of Christ." (Rev. 21:9). It is here that this promise is fulfilled because instead of running out of the city, they are snatched away, securing their safety from the earthquake. There was also an earthquake at the resurrection of Jesus Christ (Matt. 28:2). Following the earth, quake graves were opened, and people rose from the dead.

The Fig Tree

"And the stars of heaven fell unto the earth, even as a fig tree casteth her untimely figs, when she is shaken of a mighty wind" (Rev. 6:12).

This Word is rich in symbolism. The time of the figs preceded the feast of trumpets. For this reason, figs were spoken of prior to His coming, or the kingdom of God.

Here we see the figs spoken of when Jesus speaks of the end.

> "And there shall be signs in the sun, and in the moon, and in the stars; and upon the earth distress of nations, with perplexity; the sea and the waves roaring; Men's hearts failing them for fear, and for looking after those things which are coming on the earth: for the powers of Heaven shall be shaken. And then shall they see the Son of man coming in a cloud with power and great glory. And when these things begin to come to pass then look up, and lift up your heads; for your redemption draweth nigh. And he spake to them a parable; **Behold the fig tree**, and all the trees; When they now shoot forth, ye see and know of your own selves that **summer is now nigh at hand**. So likewise ye, when ye see these things come to pass, know ye that the kingdom of God is nigh at hand" (Lu. 21:25-31).

Here in Revelation, John sees the same thing as Jesus does. Isaiah speaks of this day as well:

> "And all the host of heaven shall be dissolved, and the heavens shall be rolled together as a scroll: and all their host shall fall down, as the leaf falleth off from the vine, and as a falling fig from the fig tree" (Isa. 34:4).

Jesus said, "summer is nigh at hand." He speaks of this season when he refers to the fig tree. Summer is a key to his return. Could this be what Jeremiah referred to in the chapter speaking of the wrath of God and His indignation?

> "There shall be no grapes on the vine, nor figs on the fig tree...The harvest is past, the summer is ended, and we are not saved" (Jer. 8:13,20).

This Word, "saved," is NOT referring to the salvation experience as we know it, but is about being "delivered" or "saved from impending judgment." In the Gospel of Luke, Jesus continues after speaking of the 'parable of the fig tree' with these words:

> "And take heed to yourselves, lest at any time your hearts be overcharged with surfeiting, and drunkenness, and cares of this life, and so that day come upon you unawares. For as a snare shall it come on all them that dwell on the face of the whole earth. Watch ye therefore, and pray always, that ye may be accounted worthy to escape all these things that shall come to pass..." (Lu. 21: 34-36).

However, what does the fig tree have to do with the Rapture of His Bride? Note in the Song of Solomon these words:

"The fig tree putteth forth her green figs...Arise, my love, my fair one, and come away" (Sng 2:13).

The exciting thing about this verse and Revelation 6:12 is that this is the ONLY time where figs are in the feminine tense. Something has changed. Why does John say "her figs?" Here the Church is identified as a Bride. There is no reference in the seven Churches of Asia in the female tense. Suddenly, at this moment, we see the female tense.

The figs mentioned here allude to the timing of the Rapture. The timing of figs occurred in the summertime, just before the feast of trumpets (symbolic of the Rapture).

The Feast Days

The word feast in Hebrew is "moed," meaning "a divine appointment." The Hebrew word for convocation is miqra, which means "a public meeting or dress rehearsal." God formulated the feast days to give us a clue of the timing of His return. Remember, in Scripture, God calls these feast days "my feasts" not just the feasts of Israel. "...even these are my feasts" (Lev. 23:2). There are seven important feast days. The first four have been fulfilled, and the last three are yet to be completed. The fig tree's time precedes the next feast day, which is the feast of trumpets.

The Feast of Trumpets

This unique feast was to be celebrated on the first day of the seventh month. It was held at a 'new moon', not just a full moon. "The falling of the figs" here in the opening of the seals tells us what feast day is ready to be fulfilled, and that is the feast of trumpets or understood as the Rosh Hashanah, or the new year. This feast is commemorated by blowing seven trumpets over 100 times, lasting two days. This day begins when there is a NEW MOON, not a FULL MOON. Usually, a feast day was announced when two witnesses reported to the Sanhedrin that a full moon had been observed, so the announcement would be made. This was different. This was a "new moon" that could not come from observation. This is what Jesus told them when they asked when the kingdom would come. He said,

"And when he was demanded of the Pharisees, when the kingdom of God should come, he answered them and said, The kingdom of God cometh not with observation" (Lu. 17:20).

What was he saying? This feast is different. It is NOT a full moon one is looking for; it is a NEW MOON.

"Blow up the trumpet in the new moon, in the time appointed, on our solemn feast day "(Psa. 81:3).

If this is true, then the Rapture's timing will coincide with this feast.

There are seven feast day celebrations. They are:

1. Passover (speaks of the death of Christ)
2. Unleavened Bread (speaks of the burial of Christ)
3. Feast of First Fruits (speaks of the Resurrection of Christ)
4. Feast of Pentecost (speaks of the birth of the Church).
5. Feast of Trumpets (speaks of the Rapture of His Bride).
6. Feast of Atonement (speaks of the Tribulation period).
7. Feast of Tabernacles (speaks of the millennial reign).

Feast Day Fulfillment

(1) Feast of Passover

"When I see the blood, I will pass over you" (Ex. 12:13).

God passed over the Hebrews when he saw the blood of the lamb. God also passes over our sins when he sees the blood of Christ.

(2) Feast of Unleavened Bread

"Unleavened bread shall be eaten seven days, and there shall no leavened bread be seen with thee, neither shall there be leaven seen with thee in all thy quarters" (Ex. 13:7).

Just as the Hebrews ate bread with no leaven removing all leaven from their dwellings, so is all sin removed from the believer in Jesus...past, present, and future.

(3) Feast of First Fruits

" Speak unto the children of Israel, and say unto them, When ye be come into the land which I give unto you, and shall reap the harvest thereof, then ye shall bring a sheaf of the first fruits of your harvest unto the priest: And he shall wave the sheaf before the LORD, to be accepted for you: on the morrow after the sabbath the priest shall wave it" (Lev. 23:10)..

The children of Israel were commanded to bring the sheaf of the first fruits of the barley harvest on the first day of the week (the day of resurrection) and wave it before the LORD.

"And ye shall count unto you from the morrow after the sabbath, from the day that ye brought the sheaf of the wave offering; seven sabbaths shall be complete: Even unto the morrow after the seventh sabbath shall ye number the fifty days; and ye shall offer a new meat offering unto the LORD.

The children of Israel were to count 50 days after the firstfruits sheaf of barley was waved. Then they were to offer a new wheat offering: 2 loaves of fine flour from the new harvest of wheat, *baked with leaven* and waved by the priest.

The Death of Jesus

Jesus was the sinless Lamb of God who came and gave his life so that we could have eternal life. The Burial of Jesus and our Sin

As the Baptism ceremony implies, we were buried with Jesus and our sins were buried with Him. When he rose, we also rose with Him.

The Resurrection of Jesus

In Old Testament times, the promised land was a picture of the kingdom of the Messiah. Jesus was the first to rise from the dead and after Him all that is Christ's. The resurrection of the believer in Jesus is God's promise.

"Christ our Passover is sacrificed for us" (I Cor. 5:7).

"Behold the Lamb of God, which taketh away the world's sin" (Jn. 1:29).

"Therefore we were buried with Him by baptism into death: that like as Christ was raised up from the dead by the glory of the Father, even so, we also should walk in newness of life" (Ro. 6:4).

"Therefore let us keep the feast, not with old leaven, neither with the leaven of malice and wickedness; but with the unleavened bread of sincerity and truth" (I Cor. 5:8).

"But now is Christ risen from the dead, [and] become the firstfruits of them that slept. For since by man [came] death, by man [came] also the resurrection of the dead. For as in Adam all die, even so in Christ shall all be made alive. But every man in his own order: Christ the firstfruits; afterward they that are Christ's at his coming" (I Co. 15:20-23).

"Now you are the body of Christ, and members individually" (I Cor. 12:27).

(4) Feast of Pentecost

> *"And ye shall count unto you from the morrow after the sabbath, from the day that ye brought the sheaf of the wave offering; seven sabbaths shall be complete: Even unto the morrow after the seventh sabbath shall ye number the fifty days; and ye shall offer a new meat offering unto the LORD" (Lev. 23:15-16).*

The children of Israel were to count 50 days after the first fruits sheaf of barley was waved. Then they were to offer a new wheat offering: 2 loaves of fine flour from the new wheat harvest, baked with leaven and waved by the priest.

(5) Feast of Trumpets

> *"Speak unto the children of Israel, saying, In the seventh month, in the first day of the month, shall ye have a sabbath, a memorial of blowing of trumpets, an holy convocation" (23:24).*

Trumpets were used to call the children of Israel to assemble for a meeting with the LORD. The trumpet was the signal for the workers to come into the Temple. The High Priest stood on the Temple's southwest parapet and blew the trumpet so that it could be heard in the surrounding fields. At that instant, the faithful would stop harvesting, even if there were crops, and leave immediately for the worship service.

The Birth of the Church

Fifty days after Jesus rose from the dead, the Church was born on the Day of Pentecost. This marked the end of the "Jewish Era" and the beginning of the "Church Age," where both Jews and Gentiles (2 loaves) could confess Jesus as LORD and be saved. The Announcement of Jesus' Return

The Announcement of Jesus' Return

> *"Blow ye the trumpet in Zion, and sound an alarm in my holy mountain: let all the inhabitants of the land tremble: for the day of the LORD cometh, for [it is] nigh at hand" (Joel 2:1).*

The Feast of Trumpets speaks of a time when the trumpet of the LORD will sound, and all who are in Christ will rise to Heaven. Israel will be gathered into their land, and there will be great tribulation as never before. Then the LORD Jesus will return to receive his kingdom.

> *"And when the day of Pentecost was fully come, they were all with one accord in one place. And suddenly there came a sound from Heaven as of a rushing mighty wind, and it filled all the house where they were sitting. And there appeared unto them cloven tongues*

like as of fire, and it sat upon each of them. And they were all filled with the Holy Ghost, and began to speak with other tongues, as the Spirit gave them utterance" (Acts 2:1-4).

"For as the body is one and has many members, and all the members of the body, being many, are one body; so also is Christ. For in one Spirit we were all baptized into one body, whether Jews or Greeks, whether bond or free; and were all given to drink into one Spirit" (I Cor. 12:12,13).

"And he shall send his angels with a great sound of a trumpet, and they shall gather together his elect from the four winds, from one end of heaven to the other" (Mat. 24:31).

"For the Lord, Himself shall descend from heaven with a shout, with the voice of the archangel, and with the trump of God; and the dead in Christ shall rise first" (I Thess. 4:16).

"In a moment, in the twinkling of an eye, at the last trump: for the trumpet shall sound, and the dead shall be raised incorruptible, and we shall be changed" (I Cor. 15:51).

(6) Feast of Atonement

> *"Also on the tenth day of this seventh month there shall be a day of atonement: it shall be an holy convocation unto you; and ye shall afflict your souls, and offer an offering made by fire unto the LORD" (Lev. 23:27).*

This feast was the only day that required fasting, and they were to afflict their souls, and when the high priest sprinkled the blood on the mercy seat, the sins of Israel were covered for another year. This was Israel's most significant day of the year, but its significance pointed to the atoning sacrifice of Jesus Christ, who would die on the cross for all humanity.

Afflicting their Souls speaks about the day when there will be great mourning over piercing their Messiah:

> *"And they will look to Me whom they have pierced; and they shall mourn for him, as one mourns for his only son, and will grieve bitterly for him, as one grieves for his firstborn" (Ze. 12:10).*

(7) Feast of Tabernacles (Booths)

> *"Speak unto the children of Israel, saying, The fifteenth day of this seventh month shall be the feast of tabernacles for seven days unto the LORD" (Lev. 23:34).*

The Feast of Tabernacles was the last of the LORD's feasts, commemorating the harvest's ingathering at the year's end. The prophetic fulfillment of this feast is the Millennium, the one-thousand-year reign of Jesus Christ on the earth.

The Purging of Israel's Unbelief

> *"Alas! for that day is great, so that none is like it. It is even the time of Jacob's trouble"* (Je. 30:7).

The rulers of Israel did not recognize the LORD when he came, as was predicted by all the prophets. In their rejection of their Messiah, the "Day of Atonement" was pointing to a coming day of purging, called by Jeremiah "the time of Jacob's trouble" when they would learn by "great tribulation" to say "blessed is He who comes in the name of the LORD." This is also referred to as the 70th Week of Daniel. After they "afflict their souls," he will save them.

> *"And then the sign of the Son of Man will appear in the sky. Then all the tribes of the earth will mourn, and they will see the Son of Man coming on the clouds of the sky with power and great glory"* (Mat. 24:30).

The Coming of Jesus and his Kingdom

The Feast of Tabernacles speaks of a time when Jesus will return and set up his kingdom on the earth. He will reign in Jerusalem for 1,000 years. Satan will be bound, and the joy of the LORD will fill the whole earth.

> *"For then shall be great tribulation, such as was not since the beginning of the world to this time, no, nor ever shall be" (Mat. 24:21).*

> *"For I tell you, you will not see me from now on, until you say, 'Blessed is he who comes in the name of the Lord" (Mat. 23:39).*

> *"But Christ having come as a high priest of the coming good things, through the greater and more perfect tabernacle, not made with hands, that is to say, not of this creation, nor yet through the blood of goats and calves, but his own blood, entered in once for all into the Holy Place, having obtained eternal redemption" (He. 9:11,12)..*

> *"And then shall appear the sign of the Son of man in heaven: and then shall all the tribes of the earth mourn, and they shall see the Son of man coming in the clouds of heaven with power and great glory" (Mat. 24:30).*

> *"For the Son of Man will come in the glory of his Father with his angels, and then he will render to everyone according to his deeds" (Mat. 16:27).*

It is easy to miss the Rapture of the Church as one reads the cataclysmic events unfold, but that is why figurative language is used. One must understand that these two events are happening at the very same time. That is why the language itself is used while describing these signs in the heavens. Jesus Himself, as described earlier, said there would be these signs in the heavens, and when they occurred to "look up, for your redemption draweth nigh."

What other "signs" points us to the Rapture?

The Dew

This is a very descriptive word that brings both separation and insulation into view. Isaiah tells the Bride, at that moment of cataclysmic chaos,

> *"Thy dead men shall live, together with my dead body shall they arise. Awake and sing, ye that dwell in dust:* **thy dew is the dew of herbs**, *and the earth shall cast out the dead. Come, my people, enter thou into thy chambers, and shut thy doors about thee: hide*

thyself as it were for a little moment, until the indignation be overpast" (Isa. 26:19,20).

The Bride will be both insulated from the wrath of God and separated while in the chamber with Him. The dew is symbolic of this. The presence of the Bridegroom reveals dew. Note what is said in the book of Solomon about dew.

"I sleep, but my heart wakes: it is the voice of my beloved that knocks, saying, Open to me, my sister, my love, my dove, my undefiled: for my head is filled with dew, and my locks with the drops of the night" (Song 5:2).

When Gideon tested God with the fleece, he told God to make the fleece wet and everything around it dry, and then the next night to make the fleece dry and everything around it wet. Why? He wanted to know that he (the fleece) would be insulated from what was around him in battle because he knew it was 'normal' to die, but if God were with him, he would be insulated from the effects of the war. (Judges 6:37-49). Another example was the manna placed on the dew when God brought angel food to the Israelites. This manna was 'separated' and insulated from the earth because the manna rested on the dew, not the earth. Notice what Jesus said about this manna in the Gospel of John.

> "Then Jesus said unto them, Verily, verily, I say unto you, Moses gave you not that bread from Heaven; but my Father gives you the true bread from Heaven... Moreover, this is the will of Him that sent me, that everyone which sees the Son, and believes on Him, may have everlasting life: and **I will raise him up at the last day**" (Jn. 6:31-40).

The Bride is taken to the chamber where she is insulated from the Tribulation; just as the fleece was insulated from the dew and the earth.

Finally, Jesus Himself speaks of the manna, which rested on the dew (Nu. 11:9).

> "Your fathers did eat manna in the wilderness and are dead. This is the bread which cometh down from Heaven, that a man may eat thereof, and not die. I am the living bread which came down from Heaven: if any man eat of this bread, he shall live forever: and the bread that I will give is my flesh, which I will give for the life of the world...Then Jesus said unto them, Verily, verily, I say unto you, Except ye eat the flesh of the Son of man, and drink his blood, ye have no life in you. Whoso eateth my flesh, and drinketh my blood, hath eternal life; and **I will raise him up at the last day**" (Jn. 6:49-54).

Of course, Jesus is the manna, speaking of eternal life. By extension, we know that the manna rested on the dew, so by connecting the dots, we can know that dew relates to the raising up of His believers on the last day. Jesus did NOT say 'last days' because this is a specific day that He is referring to: The day of the Rapture of His Bride.

The New Moon

The new moon shares the time of the feast of trumpets and the Rapture of the Church. The moon turning into blood is about the new moon. In Scripture, the new moon is spoken of about this feast. It was a feast to purge Israel of their sins for that year; and was their most important feast. There is a story in the Scriptures of a specific thing that happened during this period. This narrative in the Bible relates to the "new moon" and the Rapture of His Bride. David is the main character, and as seen in the book of Revelation regarding the Church of Philadelphia, David plays a key role. David, in this example, is "escaping" from Saul, who seeks to kill him. David notes this upcoming feast day and tells Jonathan, Saul's son, of his plan not to be present. Jonathan replies:

"Then Jonathan said to David, To morrow is the new moon: and **thou shalt be missed, because thy seat will be empty**" (II Sa. 20:18).

Similarly, at the time of the new moon, we, the Bride of Christ, will be missed because our seats will be "empty."

In another example, we find the prophet Ezekiel revealing the eastern gate (symbolic of His coming) opened at the new moon.

> *"Thus saith the Lord GOD; The gate of the inner court that looketh toward the east shall be shut the six working days; but on the sabbath it shall be opened, and in the day of the new moon it shall be opened"* *(Ezk. 46:1).*

Jesus is coming back from the direction of the "eastern skies." At the time of the new moon, a door "is opened." Jesus told the Church of Philadelphia, "Behold, I have set before you an open door" (Rev. 3:8). The "new moon" is also the timing of the "open door."

At the same time, the "new moon" marks the beginning of the Tribulation as spoken of in Joel.

> *"The sun shall be turned into darkness, and the moon into blood, before the great and the terrible day of the LORD come"* *(Joel 2:31).*

Those who remain will be asking when this day will be over so that they can continue their wickedness. They know that their deeds are exposed while the light shines forth, but when summer is over and the new moon is gone, they have free reign to do as they please. The prophet Amos was given a vision of 'summer fruit' to illustrate this point.

> *"Hear this, O ye that swallow up the needy, even to make the poor of the land to fail, Saying, When will the new moon be gone, that we may sell corn? and the sabbath, that we may set forth wheat, making the ephah small, and the shekel great, and falsifying the balances by deceit" (Amos 8:4,5)?*

During this time, there is a plentiful draught, not of food or water, but of the Word of God. The reason is that God's people are gone. Remember, Paul tells us we are "epistles read of all men." In the same manner that Jesus was the Word of God, we have taken on Christ, and the Word of God abides in us. It was the Word of God that John was engaged in when Jesus spoke to him in Revelation Chapter one. We know this because when he turned to see the voice speaking to him, he saw Jesus amid the candlesticks. The candlesticks were facing opposite the shewbread table, which symbolized God's Word. The Bride of Christ is filled with the Word of God

Chapter Ten

Are We Ready?

Not to bring condemnation to anyone or suggest that we are NOT ready for his appearing; the Bible points out that the Bride of Christ has "made herself ready."

> *"Let us be glad and rejoice, and give honor to Him: for the marriage of the Lamb is come, and **his wife hath made herself ready"** (Rev. 19:6).*

One of the proofs for believing in the Rapture of the Bride is that she makes herself ready. How? Paul wrote that Jesus will one day present a "Bride without spot or wrinkle unto Himself."

> *"That he might present it to Himself a glorious church, not having spot, or wrinkle, or any such thing; but that it should be holy and without blemish" (Eph. 5:25-27).*

This narrative clearly shows that Jesus has done everything He can to make His Bride presentable. Note that the Church in this passage has done absolutely nothing. It is all Jesus. Being ready is made possible through what He has done in our lives, not by what we have done. Also, the Church is referred to as "it," not "her." When the Church loves Jesus back, she becomes her, not just it. When the Church chooses to love Him back, we have a Bride, not just a church. It is here that Jesus is defining the nature of the Bride. The Bride comes from the Church that Jesus has cleansed and washed through His Word. Jesus dying on the cross was an act of love. John, the writer of Revelation, shows us how this love works in relationship to His coming.

> *"Behold, what manner of love the Father hath bestowed upon us, that we should be called the sons of God: therefore the world knoweth us not, because it knew Him not. Beloved, now are we the sons of God, and it doth not yet appear what we shall be: but we know that , when he shall appear, we shall be like Him; for we shall see Him as He is. And every man that hath this hope in him purifieth himself, even as He is pure" (I Jn 3:1-3).*

The context of both of these verses is love. Paul said that Christ loved the Church, and John also speaks of this life-changing thing called love.

What does it mean to purify ourselves, and how do we do this? The key is that the focus is NOT on us but Him. "Even as He is pure" cannot be overlooked. We will not be pure if we look on ourselves, but when our gaze is on Him, we become like Him, for "we see Him as He is." As the Shulamite woman declared, "you are altogether lovely." When it comes to cleansing sin, we are told what to do in the book of Hebrews.

> *"Wherefore seeing we also are compassed about with so great a cloud of witnesses, let us lay aside every weight, and the sin which doth so easily beset us, and let us run with patience the race that is set before us, Looking unto Jesus the author and finisher of our faith…" (Heb. 12:1,2).*

The way we become pure is to focus on the pure one. We give honor unto Him, and that is how we make ourselves ready for His appearing. One will never go wrong giving all their attention to Jesus. We become like Him when we see Him.

When we focus on our works instead of Him, we can easily be like those that Jesus said He did not know.

> *"Many will say to me in that day, Lord, Lord, have we not prophesied in thy name? And in thy name have cast out devils? And in thy name done many wonderful works? And then will I profess unto them, I never knew*

you; depart from me, ye that work iniquity" (Mt. 7:22-23).

Jesus does not need the Church to tell Him about their works because He already knows. He said to all of the seven Churches of Asia, "I know thy works...but." When we focus more on what He does and less on what we do, we will be much more fruitful because it will have been in His will, and He will receive the praise and the glory.

It is an affront to Christ Himself to suggest that a person's works are needed because His works were insufficient. It is the Christo-centric principle. All things are in Christ, and upon that rock, we stand; all other ground is sinking sand.

This author is NOT suggesting that we sit back and do nothing. It is THROUGH our faith that we show our works. Without faith, it is impossible to please Him. James makes it clear that true faith produces works:

"Even so faith, if it hath not works, is dead, being alone. Yea, a man may say, Thou hast faith, and I have works: shew me thy faith without thy works, and I will shew thee my faith by my works. Thou believest that there is one God; thou doest well: the devils also believe, and tremble. But wilt thou know, O vain man, that faith without works is dead" (Ja. 2:17-20)

James gives Abraham, the Father of faith, as an example of faith. Abraham believed in God and obeyed God by being willing to kill his son. Our works come from faith, not the other way around.

Chapter Ten

The Reward

The greatest reward will be that we are with the one we love—the meeting of the Bride with the Bridegroom. The longing and yearning is over. We can now rejoice and be glad that the marriage of the lamb has come!

We are not only escaping, as some people teach, concerning the Rapture of His Bride; we are consummating the love affair that has been going on for a very long time. We know that the Rapture of His Bride is more than escaping the Tribulation because "the dead in Christ rise first". Those that have died have nothing to escape. They are dead. We meet them in the air and are brought into the bridal "chamber" together with the Lord. In essence, this is another reward that we will be with those whom we loved while on this earth, and NOW we will meet them in the air…what a nice reunion this will be. And what a nice reward.

Apostle Paul reminds us of a crown waiting for us when we arrive. A crown is appropriate because we will be His Bride and "Queen."

> "Henceforth there is laid up for me a crown of righteousness, which the Lord, the righteous judge, shall give me at that day: and not to me only, but unto all them also that love his appearing" (II Tim. 4:8).

Apostle Peter confirms this, adding that it will be permanent.

> "And when the chief Shepherd shall appear, ye shall receive a crown of glory that fadeth not away" (I Pe. 5:4).

Finally, Jesus speaks to the Church of Philadelphia with an admonition to stand fast, loving His appearing and protecting the crown from being taken.

> "Behold, I come quickly: hold that fast which thou hast, that no man take thy crown" (Rev. 3:11).

What did Jesus mean by: "hold that fast?" He is not asking a person to have something they do NOT have, but He is saying to keep what they already have. He is saying to hold fast to the "promise" that He is coming back for His Bride. Strong's Concordance says this: "not to discard or let go; to keep carefully and faithfully." He gives us a treasure to hold. The ONLY way for someone to take "your crown" is for YOU to "discard" it and "let it go." No one has the power to take it, but a person has the choice to throw it away. Vine's Concordance suggests this:

"metaphorically, of "laying hold of the hope of the Lord's return," Hbr 6:18"

Paul put it this way:

"I have fought a good fight, I have finished my course, I have kept the faith: Henceforth there is laid up for me a crown..." (II Tim. 4:7,8).

Apostle Paul "kept" the faith. He held on firmly to what he had been entrusted. This word that Paul selected to use (tereo, τηρέω) also means: "to stay in the state you are currently in." Metaphorically, that state is "unmarried." He is reserving himself for the marriage yet to come— The Bride of Christ and the groom, Jesus Himself. He wants us to stay "unmarried" to the world and kept in the state He brought us into when he redeemed us. This is how Paul saw himself when he stated he "kept the faith." It was the same with the Church of Philadelphia, and as such, because they firmly held on and "kept" His Word, they were kept from the Tribulation that Jesus said would come upon all the earth.

> "Because thou hast kept the word of my patience, I also will keep thee from the hour of temptation, which shall come upon all the world, to try them that dwell upon the earth" (Rev. 3:8).

"kept" also denotes observing his commandments and, by extension, "keeping them." Could there be a correlation between keeping His commandments, or sayings, and the Rapture? Look at what Jesus said about this:

> "Verily, verily, I say unto you, If a man keep my saying, he shall never see death" (Jn. 8:51).

They highly criticized Jesus for this statement, and this statement had a 'knee-jerk' reaction. They even wanted to kill him for making this statement. Upon face value, this verse is interpreted by Scholars as a "spiritual death." This is the accepted view and is mine also. However, could He have been saying more than this? Jesus does not explain here, but elsewhere in other Gospels he does:

> "Verily I say unto you, There be some standing here, which shall not taste of death, till they see the Son of man coming in his kingdom" (Mt. 16:28).

"But I tell you of a truth, there be some standing here, which shall not taste of death, till they see the kingdom of God" (Lu. 9:27).

Whom was He referring? One possibility is that He was referring to John, who saw Jesus and His coming kingdom before John physically saw death. John happens to record this account after Jesus met with the disciples before His accession into Heaven.

> *"Then Peter, turning about, seeth the disciple whom Jesus loved following; which also leaned on his breast at supper, and said, Lord, which is he that betrayeth thee? Peter seeing him saith to Jesus, Lord, and what shall this man do? Jesus saith unto him, If I will that he tarry till I come, what is that to thee? follow thou me. Then went this saying abroad among the brethren, that that disciple should not die: yet Jesus said not unto him, He shall not die; but, If I will that he tarry till I come, what is that to thee"* (Jn. 21:21-23).

In conclusion, the fact that Jesus precedes these words with 'verily, verily' makes it more serious. When Jesus told the Church of Philadelphia to "hold fast" that which they have and let "no man take your crown," we should also heed. This author's final words are the same as John's final words in the final book of the Bible:

"He which testifieth these things saith, Surely I come quickly. Amen. Even so, come, Lord Jesus" (Rev. 22:20).

The Rapture of His Bride — Opening of the Sixth Seal & The Blood Moon Cataclysmic Events

Scriptural Evidence for Believing in the Rapture

Timothy R. Gilbert, MA

www.ingramcontent.com/pod-product-compliance
Lightning Source LLC
Chambersburg PA
CBHW072337300426
44109CB00042B/1650